MARTINSON MIDDLE SCHOOL
LIBRARY
Marshfield. Mass. 02050

W9-AAG-051

WOMEN IN MEDICINE

THIS MONUMENT WAS ERECTED IN 1938
AND REDEDICATED IN 1971
TO COMMEMORATE DEVOTED SERVICE
TO COUNTRY AND HUMANITY BY
ARMY, NAVY AND AIR FORCE NURSES

WOMEN IN MEDICINE

by Hedda Garza

WOMEN THEN–WOMEN NOW

FRANKLIN WATTS
New York   Chicago   London   Toronto   Sydney

Frontispiece:
The white marble sculpture of a nurse in uniform stands
in Arlington National Cemetery, a memorial to the army,
navy, and air force nurses who served in World War I.

30020000146173 Q

Cover illustration copyright ©: Lisa Steinberg
Photographs copyright ©: Jay Mallin: p. 2; The Bettmann Archive: pp. 16, 41,
45, 49, 99, 105; Schlesinger Library, Radcliffe College: p. 67; Wide World
Photos: pp. 72, 74, 82, 121; Howard University Hospital/Jay Mallin: pp. 93,
134; UPI/Bettmann Newsphotos: p. 110; The American Red Cross: p. 115.

Library of Congress Cataloging-in-Publication Data

Garza, Hedda.
    Women in medicine / by Hedda Garza.
        p.   cm. – (Women then—women now)
    Includes bibliographical references and index.
    ISBN 0-531-11204-7 (lib. bdg.)
        1. Women in medicine—History—Juvenile literature.   [1. Women in
medicine—History.   2. Medicine—History.]   I. Title.   II. Series.
R692.G37   1994
610'.82–dc20   94-21034 CIP AC

920
B
GAR

17039

Copyright © 1994 by Hedda Garza
All rights reserved
Printed in the United States of America
6 5 4 3 2 1

CONTENTS

*For my son, Danny,
who so long ago fought alongside me
to change the world.*

few points above the zero mark, it would remain stuck there for many more decades.

A separate graph of women physicians in the United States would also show a low horizontal line from the American Revolution right through the Civil War, when women were barred from most medical schools. Suddenly, near the end of the nineteenth century the line would shoot up, representing the fact that one-fourth or more of the newly graduated doctors were women.

Around 1910, women again strangely vanished from the classrooms of U.S. medical schools. Soon they filled less than 3 percent of the classroom seats.[2] Although women were accepted as nurses, women physicians remained a rarity until very recent times, when once again the graph line climbed upward, women in medicine edging toward the one-third mark.

Will the line on our graph plunge down again or will it stay put? If we want to know the future, we have to uncover the secrets behind the suddenly opening and closing doors that barred and then admitted women to the world of healing. Our investigation must begin in ancient times.

Digging in the ruins of buried civilizations, archaeologists have unearthed evidence of flourishing civilizations that held women healers in high esteem long before recorded history.[3] More than 5,000 years ago, in the city-state of Sumer, Mesopotamia, close to present-day Iraq, a hymn of praise was sung to the goddess Ishtar: "Where you cast your glance, the dead awaken, the sick arise."[4] For almost three thousand years, Sumerian women used plant extracts to reduce pain, heal, and disinfect. Women surgeons operated with flint and bronze tools. In about 2600 B.C., foreign tribes invaded and crushed the Sumerian defenders. Blaming the goddesses for their defeat, the hungry and diseased populace prayed to male warrior gods instead. With their importance diminished, women were eventually banned from educational institutions. By around 1000 B.C., they were no longer listed as scribes and doctors. Only a few nurses and midwives remained as helpers to the all-male medical profession.

The legacy of earlier Sumerian medicine traveled over the trade routes to other civilizations. In burial mounds high on the hillsides of Denmark, the bones of thirty high priestesses from the Bronze Age were found with surgical implements and recipes for healing herbs alongside their remains.

During spring rituals in Scandinavia, sacrifices were made to female deities, especially to Nerthus, goddess of fertility. This time the unstable forces of nature, rather than war, dislodged women from their lofty positions. As glaciers of the ice age moved closer, seas flooded the lands, the climate chilled, and many hungry people fled. When other tribes invaded and conquered the weakened Danes, the goddesses of the Danes were again replaced by male gods of war. After many centuries, the goddess Nerthus was resurrected as the goddess Freyja, and once again women were respected for their healing powers. This culture survived over the centuries in the Scandinavian countries, which have led the world in establishing women's rights.

Far from Scandinavia, among the ancient Aztecs of Mexico, the native Americans in North America, the tribes of the Pacific Islands, in China, and in Siam, women also worked as healers, midwives, and hospital surgeons before 1000 B.C. Most of the women were pushed out by men with the arrival of hard times.

The medical school at Heliopolis, Egypt, admitted women as early as 1500 B.C. In Greece, many women healers were included in the pantheon of gods. Helen of Troy, who lived around 2000 B.C., was renowned for her healing skills. The Hippocratic oath, still sworn to by physicians today, pays homage to the goddesses of prevention and cure with the words: "I swear by . . . Hygeia and Panacea."[5] *Panacea* is today's English word for cure-all.

As the Roman hordes invaded, the women in Greece

also lost their status. By 460 B.C., they were working as assistants to male physicians and were barred from midwifery as well. A few brave women practiced medicine in secret and even wrote medical texts, which were later attributed to men. One woman, Agnodice, around 300 B.C., was arrested for disguising herself as a man in order to practice medicine. She won her liberty when a group of prominent Athenian women appeared at her trial and threatened to sexually boycott their husbands if Agnodice was imprisoned.

After the Romans finally conquered Greece in 146 B.C. and enslaved the Greeks, Greek women healers were sold at top prices in the Roman slave market because Greek women taught their skills to their new mistresses. Until then, Roman "doctoring" had consisted of prayers to goddesses in charge of curing various diseases. Pliny, a famous writer and administrator in the first century A.D., warned Roman women who studied Greek medicine to keep silent about their achievements. Perhaps as a result, only a few women left records of their medical knowledge.

While Roman woman healers quietly cared for the sick, the so-called Fathers of Medicine wrote medical books. Galen, the most famous, produced over five hundred books in the fourth century A.D. His theory that an imbalance of the body's four fluids—blood, phlegm, and black and yellow bile—caused all illness dominated medical thinking until the nineteenth century.

Meanwhile, in the second century A.D., Rome's power began to decline. Diseases and malaria from the surrounding swamps seeped into congested cities, causing panic and death. Prominent among those who selflessly tended the sick and dying were the earliest followers of Jesus Christ, many of them women. As the Roman leaders escalated their persecution of Christians, many of the popular women healers were captured and put to death. Fabiola, a friend of Saint Jerome, managed to evade capture and continue her work. She founded the first public hospital in Europe in 394 A.D., a refuge for the poor and homeless. Her friend Paula opened a similar hospital for the Jews. The women had very few male supporters among the Christians. Even Saint Jerome, who had praised Fabiola and other Christian healers, condemned women as "the path of wickedness, the sting of the serpent . . . a perilous object."[6]

The Dark Ages followed the fall of Rome in 476 A.D. and lasted more than six hundred years. The dreaded bubonic plague swept across the continent with terrifying speed, borne by infected fleas and spread by invading and migrating tribes. Most victims died of hemorrhaging within three days. Civilization disintegrated as people fled from towns and cities.

In the rural areas, where over three-quarters of Europe's population lived, the squalid huts of the peasants and the feudal castles of the lords had no water or sanitary facilities. City dwellings were even worse. They were perfect breeding places for disease. Women gave birth year after year, with half their children dying before the age of twenty. As libraries were looted and burned by rampaging mobs, ancient medical books were lost. Women healers relied on magical potions composed of animal feces, saliva, dead insects, and other useless and often harmful ingredients.

Between 1000 and 1300 A.D., Europe began a slow recovery. As the waves of disease and invasions slowed, land was cleared for crops, and cities were built. Social-class divisions sharpened. The landowning nobility and many churchmen enjoyed the luxuries of the time, such as a portable toilet or a fireplace with vents. With a healthier environment, now many of their illnesses—high blood pressure, gout, and heart disease—were caused by gluttony.

The serfs who produced the oversupply at the nobles' dinner tables remained wretchedly poor. Leprosy and other dread diseases spread like wildfire among them. In France alone there were two thousand leper colonies.

Managers of the nobles' estates, merchants, artisans, and craftspeople formed a new middle class. Middle-class women worked in family trades and as teachers, midwives, barbers, lacemakers, and seamstresses.

Medical care remained almost nonexistent until Arab scholars in the eleventh century translated the works of Galen, Aristotle, and Hippocrates into Arabic, and Jewish scholars retranslated them into Latin and took them west. These new textbooks formed a basis for schools to train physicians. The most famous school was at Salerno, Italy. Officially founded by Constantinus Africanus in 1075, it remained open until Napoleon ordered it shut in 1811. Although the student body and faculty were coed, women were not permitted to earn the doctor of medicine degree.

The medical writings of Trotula, a woman professor at Salerno, are on display in European museums. Despite many superstitions included in her books, Trotula's theories were so advanced for her time that later scholars argued over their authenticity. Trotula recommended pulse readings and urine studies as diagnostic tools, and she was amazingly familiar with cesarean sections and the use of opiates for anesthesia during surgery. Although the role of bacteria as the source of infection was unknown, Trotula insisted that cleanliness was related to good health, and she demanded it in operating rooms.

The instructions in her book on gynecology were followed for hundreds of years, including, we can assume, a famous "recipe" for counterfeiting virginity that included a regime of astringent soaks and suppositories. It began and then ended with the following words:

> This remedy will be needed by any girl who has been induced to open her legs and lose her virginity by the follies of passion, secret love, and promises. . . . Best of all, is this deception: the day before her marriage, let her put a leech very cau-

tiously on the labia . . . then she should allow
blood to trickle out and form a crust on the orifice
. . . thus may a false virgin deceive a man in
intercourse.[7]

Other medical schools were founded by graduates of Salerno, but few accepted women as students. A breakthrough for women healers came ironically during a killing spree, as it would time after time in the future. The Roman Catholic church launched a Holy War, the Crusades, to Christianize the unwilling populations of other lands. The First Crusade alone claimed over 800,000 lives! Men and women raced to join the parade, attracted by the pope's promise of absolution for those who undertook the dangerous mission.

As men lay wounded and dying, makeshift clinics were set up in Jerusalem and along the march route through Europe. Male doctors recruited from Church-based medical orders commanded armies of nurses, often nuns.

In 1125, the Church decided that monks should concentrate on religious studies, and they were barred from performing most medical tasks. Bone setting, bleeding, wound treating, and dental extractions were performed by barbers, tradespeople, and 200,000 women. Many had learned their skills as nurses during the early Crusades.

At the end of the thirteenth century, medical men began to form guilds to shut out those who did not meet their criteria. In reality, their methods were no better than those of the women and men they excluded. As in the days of Rome, superstition remained the key ingredient of all treatment plans. Instead of old amulets and animal parts, souvenirs from the Crusades—scrapings from gravestones, waters from shrines—were used to heal wounds and drive away illness.

In the next few centuries, almost all women healers

This drawing is of a nun of the order of Hospitalers.
The women of this order were nurses in the hospital of
St. John of Jerusalem during the Crusades. In the medieval
period, women in religious orders practiced the healing
arts. At the same time, male authorities often accused
women healers of witchcraft.

were nuns and abbesses. Fleeing from a predictable future of multiple pregnancies and virtual enslavement by tyrannical husbands, women from every social class chose life in the Church. As nuns, many of them were permitted to travel and study.

From early times, some abbesses concentrated on studying the healing arts. Hildegard of Bingen (1098–1179), the best-known abbess of the Middle Ages, recommended a treatment for diabetes that emphasized the elimination of sweets from the diet. But the Church fathers were intolerant. In 1022 they instituted the first Holy Inquisition with a trial at Orleans, France, of one small sect, the Cathers. The Cathers had made the mistake of permitting women to serve as preachers and teachers. Pope Innocent III ordered the Albigensian Crusade against the Cathers. Twenty years of persecution and executions wiped them out, fattening Church coffers by seizing the possessions of the "heretics."

As women, ever more intimidated by the Inquisition, turned their dowries over to the Church fathers instead of to their future husbands, the Church bought up one-third of the land of Europe. This led to growing criticism of abuses of wealth and power. The clerics moved quickly to crush the rising tide of opposition, especially among the land-starved peasants.

Only a trickle of laywomen practiced medicine in Europe, but they were very popular among the peasant families they treated. Churchmen suspected that these women practitioners were stirring up trouble. Church writings increasingly emphasized the evil of woman as the descendant of the treacherous Eve.

The fifteenth-century Inquisition slaughtered millions, with women healers as its prized targets. The ground for this incredible witch-hunt was fertilized by several philosophers, still reverently studied in today's universities as the so-called forefathers of science. Men like Sir Roger Bacon and Saint Thomas Aquinas were all members of religious orders or high-placed clergymen. With the good intention of sorting out superstition from genuine science, they categorized various practices as either the work of God or the work of the devil (often a woman). Bacon explained what we today call the "power of suggestion" as the magic of magicians, witches, "old wives" and wizards, aided by demons, capable of influencing the mind of another person through use of the "evil eye." Aquinas warned that those using herbs and words must be watched closely.[8]

Once again natural disasters and war paved the way for a major onslaught against women. In the early fourteenth century, glaciers advanced, bringing bitter winters and severe famine to a population that had tripled in three centuries. The Hundred Years' War between France and England started when starving bands raided French towns in 1346. In the fall of 1347, another terrible plague, the Black Death, spread through Europe, killing close to half the population. The hungry survivors became more vulnerable to disease and succumbed to syphilis, leprosy, and measles. Physicians, helpless to combat the plague, fled, carrying the disease still further.

For the next century the turmoil of internal and external wars swept over the continent. Often, the Church, with its high taxes, was blamed for the misery and poverty. Peasants burned effigies of cardinals and even the pope. Some dared to refuse to work Church lands.

With desperately ill and wounded people everywhere, there simply were not enough physicians to take care of them all. In 1352, the French king John the Good permitted women who passed an examination to practice medicine. Women healers studied medicine and practiced in England until 1422, when medical education was officially closed to them by an act of Parliament.

In 1511, King Henry VIII, a famous glutton, established the all-male College of Physicians and Surgeons and gave it the sole right to issue medical licenses throughout the entire country. All-male medical guilds were formed as well, the forerunners of the American Medical Association.

This did not improve medical care by one whit. The newly licensed "professionals" did not help patients any more than did the lower-cost barber-surgeons or the "tooth-drawers" performing dental extractions at county fairs. And no wonder! A medical guide used by the new elite doctors called for herbs mixed with wine, warm wrappings, and the singing of religious songs as the cure for almost all ailments.

Physicians throughout Europe occasionally trained women as their assistants, usually limiting them to delivering babies. These midwives worked under the constant threat of fines, imprisonment, and even death if a stillborn or deformed child was born to a noblewoman while they were attending her.

One Parisian midwife, Jacoba Felicie, fined many times for working on her own without a license, was brought before the Court of Justice in 1322 by the administrators of the Faculty of Medicine. These were the very men who had prevented her from taking the courses necessary to qualify for a license. Just as the women of Athens had supported Agnodice 1,600 years earlier, witnesses came forward to praise Jacoba's skills. The accused spoke eloquently about the need for women physicians, and the court decided that she could continue a limited practice, *but receive no payment!*

In Germany, in 1394, there were fifteen licensed women physicians in Frankfurt au Main, most of them trained by physician fathers. Since most male physicians refused to treat the poor, in 1406, the holy Roman emperor Sigismund appointed salaried women to take on that task.

In many parts of Europe, the female healers, sometimes called "sagas" or "wise women," with their herbal remedies and comforting care, were preferred to licensed physicians who used bleeding according to signs of the zodiac and prescribed such remedies as "moss from the skull of a hanged thief."[9] Often the saga was a neighbor of the poor people she treated. Male physicians claimed that since the wise women had not studied medicine (which they were barred from doing), the devil could be the only source of their abilities. These outrageous charges, backed by the clergy, proved a convenient way for the doctors to get rid of the competition.

As a remarkable renaissance in the arts, humanities, science and technology began in the 1400s, fresh efforts were made by the new intellectuals to encourage an atmosphere of learning and inquiry. Seeing itself once more under attack, the Church launched a fresh inquisition to destroy its enemies. This time the witch-hunt was widespread and intense. Women remained its primary victims for almost two centuries.[10]

An instruction manual on the detection of witches, *Malleus Maleficarum*, became the official guidebook for persecution. In it witch-midwives were said to "surpass all other witches in their crimes."[11] Chapters bore titles such as "Beware Old Women"; "Midwives are Wicked Witches"; "Evil Began with Eve"; and "Never Allow Women to Exercise Power."[12] Pope Innocent VIII issued a Papal bull appending *Malleus* and specifying that if a woman was able to heal without official learning, she would be condemned to death as a witch.

The woman-hating contents of *Malleus* persisted into modern times. When Reverend Montague Summers translated the *Malleus* into English in 1928, he prefaced the volume with the following words:

> *There can be no doubt that had this most excellent tribunal continued to enjoy its full prerogative and the full exercise of its salutary powers, the world at large would be in a far happier and far more orderly position to-day.[13]*

From 1479 to as late as 1735 in some places, an estimated nine million people were executed as witches or heretics. Many were healers and midwives. In some places, ten women were burned at the stake for every one male heretic.

An incredible array of charges were leveled against accused "witches." They were "inciting the minds of men to inordinate passion changing men into beasts with their magic act. . . ."[14] Midwives were accused of stealing placentas and umbilical cords for their magic and murdering infants or offering them to the devil. The more beloved and talented a midwife, the more her life was in danger.

The Church itself funded and led the Holy Inquisition. Though it was later called the Spanish Inquisition, it nevertheless spread all over Europe. First Dominican friars and later Jesuits brought in the suspects, tortured them, and then judged them. Civic authorities presided over their trials and passed sentence. To extract "confessions," the accused were doused with alcohol and set on fire, whipped, hung upside down, and had their thumbs and toes broken in vises in torture chambers financed by the Church. They would then "admit" their crimes—pacts with the devil, riding on broomsticks at night to secret meetings or orgies, desecration of the crucifix, raising storms, and even cannibalism.

Since witch finders were well paid, friends spoke out against friends, neighbors against neighbors. "Witches" were blamed for all of life's small problems, from hens that stopped laying to cows that failed to produce milk. Old or homely women were especially endangered, as we can see by the caricatures of witches every Halloween.

In his writings, Thomas Aquinas even blamed witches for male impotence, and many men took his opinion to heart. An accusation of witchcraft was often used as a way to get rid of an unwanted wife or to punish a woman who spurned a man's sexual advances. Even pets of accused women, especially black cats, were called "familiars," demons in disguise, and were burned in public squares along with their unfortunate mistresses.

In Germany alone, where the Inquisition was more severe and longer lasting, 100,000 witch burnings were documented. In about 1600, an observer noted that "Germany is almost entirely occupied with building fires for the witches . . ."[15] Three hundred children were burned for "having intercourse with the devil."[16]

Philippus Aureolus Paracelsus, a great Renaissance physician who established chemistry's role in medicine, burned his medical books in public in 1527. He declared that all of his knowledge had come from the Sorceresses.[17]

As governments strengthened their power, they moved toward acceptance of a variety of religious expression and the separation of church and state. At last, the Inquisition wound down. In England the last witch was hanged in 1684, although the American colonists in Massachusetts revived the practice in 1692. Germany held on the longest, finally outlawing witch-burning in 1775.

Although they no longer feared for their lives, women were viewed everywhere with distrust, had no citizenship rights, and suffered low status. Medically, they were allowed by law to practice midwifery only. They were also barred from the exciting new world of scientific research. In 1662, the all-male Royal Society, chartered by the English Parliament, excluded women on the grounds that they were mentally incapable.

Thus, by the time the first colonists sailed on the *Mayflower* to the New World, sexism in medicine had been officially institutionalized. The powerful life-giving goddesses of Sumeria, Denmark, and Greece had been dumped into the wastebin of history. A masculine god now revealed his secrets to a male-only fraternity of doctors and scientists.

two

BARRED DOORS IN THE NEW WORLD

No people go down until their women are weak and dishonored . . .

—From the puberty ceremony for young Sioux Indian maidens.[1]

Women making the perilous journey from Europe to the strange environment of the American colonies undoubtedly had high hopes for a new and better life. Unfortunately, their Old World heritage traveled with them. With the status of women at its lowest ebb in Western history, equality was almost unthinkable.

Because of the hardships of early Colonial life and a severe labor shortage, women actively participated in the strenuous tasks of clearing the land for crops and producing the goods necessary for survival. With only a handful of doctors in the colonies, most of them untrained or at best apprentices,[2] wives and mothers tended to the health of their families. Although they performed the same functions as the physicians, women who served as midwives and herbalists were called "domestic practitioners" or "kitchen physics." Often they traveled to far-flung settlements to deliver babies or tend to the sick.[3]

One of the most famous was Anne Hutchinson, leader of the Antinomians, a group of dissidents who dared to criticize the church leaders of the Massachusetts Bay Colony. Hutchinson met with dozens of women in her Boston home, preaching that everyday people were perfectly capable of studying the Bible on their own. She was put on trial several times, charged with the crimes of heresy, delivering a deformed baby, and challenging the authority of governor John Winthrop. Hutchinson humbled herself by submitting a long letter of apology to her judges, but they banished her anyway. A few years later, she was killed on Long Island, New York, when Indians attacked the settlers who had stolen their land.[4]

There are scant records of the few women physicians who practiced before the American Revolution. Several were surgeons, and one was even a town's official doctor—Sarah Sands of Block Island, Maine.[5] But before 1650, there were only two female doctors among seventy-six Boston-area physicians. In 1641, as the result of vague witchcraft charges, Jane Hawkins was banned from practice and exiled from Boston. Margaret Jones fared even worse. She was executed in 1648. Not surprisingly, no female physicians were listed in the area until almost two centuries later.[6]

Although the witch-hunt in the New World was never as fierce as it had been in Europe, several women were hanged and burned throughout the New England colonies. In 1692, in Boston, only four years before the famous witch-hunt in nearby Salem Village, four children were suddenly afflicted with convulsions. The doctor who failed to cure them blamed their problems on a neighbor washerwoman. The Goodwife Glover was hauled before the magistrates, tried as a witch, convicted, and hanged. The children's fits continued despite this extreme "remedy."[7]

The famous Salem events began when several young girls were also subject to violent convulsive fits, plus periods of deafness, blindness, speechlessness, choking, and hallucinations. By today's medical standards, they would probably have been diagnosed as hysterics. Again, a puzzled physician announced that the "evil hands" of witches and demons were twisting their victims' bodies. Several unconventional women were arrested. They were somewhat better off than they would have been in Europe. If they admitted to witchcraft, they were told, they would be allowed to live. Some of them confessed, but others, fearful in those very religious times that such a falsehood would bar them from heaven, refused. Nineteen women were hanged, and one died from the injuries she suffered when she was buried under heavy rocks for refusing to speak—a torture known as "pressing."[8]

The belief in witchcraft continued for many years, casting a shadow over women healers. Because modesty dictated that men, including male physicians, stay away from women during childbirth, midwifery was the only area of medicine where women were welcomed. Since many early pioneer women spent half their lives pregnant, birthing, nursing, and weaning, midwives were much in demand.

A Puritan woman in labor would be surrounded by a bevy of female relatives and friends, all supervised by a midwife. The patient was urged to bear her pains in silence as a sign of resignation to God's will. Although herbs and prayers differed from colony to colony, the methods of delivering a baby varied only in minor ways. Even among the Fox Indians and many other native American tribes, a woman gave birth in silence in an isolated shelter with her mother, mother-in-law, and a midwife present.

Licensing restrictions on midwives were introduced decades before the American Revolution, as more European-educated doctors arrived and cast envious eyes on their lost income opportunities. Many widows practiced midwifery as the only way they could earn a living. Obviously, they opposed restrictive laws designed to put them out of business. Self-trained and apprentice-trained male practitioners often agreed with the midwives, fearing that they would also face unemployment.

In Louisiana, as early as 1722, midwives were ordered to take tests before a committee of six physicians. Even those women who held diplomas from European medical schools were classified as midwives and ordered to wait for the arrival of a physician before delivering a baby! New York and several other states eventually followed suit.

Rather than ceasing to work or being placed under impossible restrictions, many midwives practiced illegally. In Philadelphia in 1765, Dr. William Shippen, Jr., probably realized that it was better to train midwives since they were determined to practice in any event. He offered a coed course in midwifery, the only one in Colonial America. Criticized by his colleagues for helping to "legitimize" inferior care, Shippen closed his makeshift school after the American Revolution and concentrated on teaching male medical students at the Philadelphia Medical School.

More successful efforts to thin out the ranks of female midwives in the colonies coincided with a virtual war against midwives in England, the mother country of many of the colonists. It started with the unveiling of a new surgical instrument—the forceps—nothing more complex than a set of tongs that could grip the emerging baby during difficult births.

Actually, the forceps had been invented in the sixteenth century by Peter Chamberlen the Elder. The male midwives of that family kept their father's miracle tool a secret and advertised that they could deliver babies with far less danger. By 1750, others had similar "extraction" tools. The all-male medical guilds moved quickly to rule that only male physicians could be trained to use such simple devices.

Convincing women to call on male midwife-physicians was no easy task. Most women and even some physicians themselves objected to men being present during labor and birth. One British doctor even suggested that male midwives wear a feminine costume!

To overcome society's resistance to male midwives, the male physicians launched a vicious propaganda war. Midwives were accused of using unscientific methods, having no knowledge of anatomy, and even amputating parts of the infants' bodies during deliveries. Even Dr. Shippen described "difficult labors, most of which were made so by the unskillful old women . . ."9 Male midwives promised women safe and comfortable "scientific" deliveries. Fear eventually proved more powerful than modesty.

In 1753, James Lloyd returned from a visit to Europe, bringing news of male midwives to the colonies. Medicine at that time promised to be a high-income profession. Delivering babies was, of course, a dependable source of income, but a rapidly expanding population also meant that many people would be seeking medical attention of all kinds.

By the beginning of the eighteenth century, 250,000 people had migrated to the New World, and by 1760, there were more than a million and a half people in the colonies.10

The self-advertising of the medical men about their safe and scientific methods was not based on reality. Despite the scientific discoveries of the Renaissance, health care changed very little until the end of the nineteenth century. In a few faraway lands such as Turkey, smallpox inoculations were already being introduced. In England and the American colonies, however, chants, purges with multiple enemas, bleeding with leeches, and use of toxic chemicals continued to be the main prescriptions for treating smallpox until Edward Jenner announced his vaccination for smallpox in 1789.

When it came to childbirth knowledge, Percivall Willoughby, a leader in the war against midwives in England, recommended that a woman hemorrhaging in childbirth drink a liquid containing hog's dung and the ashes of a toad, and that a pessary composed of the same dubious ingredients be inserted in her womb. Little wonder that as late as 1872 maternal and infant death rates in England were extremely high. Many studies showed that the women treated by midwives fared much better under their less aggressive management.[11] Native American medicine men and women thought that the harsh methods used by the Colonial physicians made no sense at all. Herbal medicines, cleansing, draining and irrigating of wounds, and careful tending of the sick were their stock in trade. The medical practices of most so-called primitive Indian tribes closely resembled those of the early European women healers. Long before syringes were included in doctors' bags, native Americans had invented them, using an animal bladder for the bulb and a hollow bone as the applicator.[12]

Advances in medicine first came in England with William Harvey's study of blood circulation and the growing use of autopsies to study the inner workings of the human body. Galen's old theories gradually lost prestige. Many apprentices in the Colonial period and after the Revolution traveled to Britain and France for medical training. When these men returned, they brought credentials as well as special obstetrical tools. Their efforts to belittle and then exclude midwives from the profession escalated. With even the "lesser" trade of midwifery being snatched away from women, there was not even a mention of the possibility of admitting women when the first American medical school was launched at the University of Pennsylvania in 1767.

Fear of the doctors eventually undercut the self-confidence of even the most skilled and popular of the midwives, women like Martha Moore Ballard of Kennebec, Maine. Ballard kept a diary from January 1785 until 1812.[13] It provided a detailed record of her life as a practitioner-midwife, the medicines she used, the illnesses she treated, and even her relationships with the male doctors of her area, many of whom depended heavily on her knowledge.

In some of Ballard's very discreet comments, her fear of persecution by male physicians can be seen. Speaking of a Dr. Cony, Ballard writes:

> He . . . accused me with going to Mr. Dingleys in his sickness and objecting to his prescriptions and prescribing some of my own and seting Mrs. Dingley Crying by giving my opinion of the disease and said this was one of many instances I had done so. Which I must deny till her or some other Can bring it to my recollection . . .[14]

Mr. Dingley apparently backed Ballard up and she seemed very relieved, but it was apparent in those early days of the new Republic that a powerful male medical elite was already beginning to take shape.

Men who had served in the Continental army's medical service or had studied in Edinburgh, the world's medical center at the time, wanted to create a medical profession in the United States. To do this, licensing standards would have to be set in order to get rid of various and assorted practitioners and midwives. Male midwives rushed to complete their medical degrees as the state governments passed laws restricting practice to those who held degrees.[15]

A minuscule number of women were still identified as doctors, indicating that they had served an apprenticeship. They worked in isolated rural areas or impoverished urban neighborhoods where no physician cared to live. Mrs. Frances Combes practiced in the 1780s, after apprenticing with Kentucky's first doctor, George Hartt. When the first male physician appeared in Bethel, Maine in 1800, a roaming "doctress" who covered areas of Maine, Vermont, and New York was very upset and apparently stopped her visits to Bethel.[16] Mary Lavinder set up a practice of midwifery and pediatrics in Savannah, Georgia in 1814 and conducted a visiting medical service for the poor. She rode through the city in a wagon drawn by an ancient white horse, bringing food and blankets for the ill, ministering to them "as doctor, nurse, housekeeper . . . and lastly comforter."[17]

These few medical women were a dying breed. It seemed there would be no replacements for them in the future.

Women were not unaware of their second-class status. When the Declaration of Independence was being drafted, Abigail Adams wrote to her husband John Adams, one of the assembled dignitaries and a future president:

> I desire you would remember the ladies, and be more generous to them than your ancestors. Do not put such unlimited power in the hands of the husbands. Remember, all men would be tyrants if they could. . . . we . . . will not hold ourselves bound to obey the laws in which we have no voice or representation.[18]

The Founding Fathers failed to include women, black people, and native Americans in their Declaration of Independence and Constitution. Except for a few short years in New Jersey, women were not permitted to vote. They worked endless hours to build America, running inns, spinning at home for newly developing factories, and later even toiling as brewers, tanners and lumber-jacks. But the pleas of early women's-rights advocates like Abigail Adams and the occasional man like Thomas Paine were mere whispers in the wind.

No longer labeled witches, women suffered instead from the misogyny (hatred of women) and sexism lodged firmly in the baggage brought over by the first colonists.

three

POUNDING ON THE DOORS

It was one of the first and happiest fruits of improved medical education in America that women were excluded from practice, and it was only by the united and persevering exertions of some of the most distinguished individuals our profession has been able to boast, that this was effected.

—Dr. Walter Channing, professor of obstetrics at Harvard Medical School in 1820.[1]

As word spread in Europe that jobs and fertile lands were waiting on the other side of the Atlantic, the population of the fledgling new Republic grew rapidly, and its borders expanded. By 1800, guns had been victorious over arrows, and 700,000 white settlers lived west of the Allegheny mountains, outnumbering the Indians eight to one. As industry mushroomed in the northeast and plantations blanketed the South, millions more arrived from Europe. By 1840, the population stood at 11 million. The young nation was an energetic economic engine.

The "Cult of Domesticity" (also called the cult of true womanhood) assigned to the women at home a supposedly glamorous role whose influence still lingers today.[2] Special status and a new twist were given to the old tasks women had always performed—childrearing, cleaning, cooking. Women were advised to limit their decisionmaking to their own sphere—the home. Men were to determine the course of worldly affairs, vote, and control family finances.

Evangelists toured the country, recruiting women to their churches and urging them to take their homemaking jobs seriously. Articles in dozens of ladies' magazines expounded on the importance of women's work and instructed their readers on the ways to provide impeccably clean and happy surroundings, take care of the sick, lead a religious life, excel at sewing and embroidery, educate children, minister to the needy.

In England, under the reign of Queen Victoria, a rigid code of morals had come into being and was transported to the New World. Victorianism, with its double standard of sexual morality, hardened into place in the New World. Placed on pedestals as queens of their own home sphere, white middle-class women were told that they were of a higher moral order than men. (Working-class women and slave women were never placed on pedestals, of course.) It was women's duty to be models of sexual purity, religious fervor, and perpetual innocence, while still managing to be alluring and feminine. Men would make every effort to seduce them, the preachers and writers warned, but a good woman must never surrender.

Women were advised to avoid sexual contact with their husbands as much as possible. Husbands, in turn, were encouraged to respect their "angels in the house" and make less frequent sexual demands. Many women, exhausted from multiple pregnancies anyway, willingly accepted the new norms. The birth rate declined as pornography and prostitution spread.

Many women, especially single, poor, and/or free black and Hispanic women, found it necessary to work for a living. Their paychecks were usually half the size of those of their male counterparts. By 1850, out of a work force of six million, half a million were women—definitely not "angels in the house." Banned from institutions of higher learning, 55,000 women taught in the elementary schools, where the wages were low but educational requirements were also minimal.

For these working-class women, the values of the Cult of Domesticity, even if desirable, were unattainable. Their labors and wages were needed before marriage to help at home and, after marriage, to feed their own children. By the 1830s and 1840s, the vast majority of female workers toiled twelve hours a day in the textile mills and other factories. Some workers were children as young as seven or eight. Instead of gasping for air from the pressure of heavily boned stays and corsets, women choked on the thick black smoke of the oil lamps that lit their workplaces. To keep them virtuous (and undoubtedly decrease absenteeism), New England employers rented them rooms in milltown dormitories, where they lived under strict rules.

Thirty thousand women, many of them immigrants working off the price of their passage, labored as maids and cooks for the middle classes and wealthy "true domestic women." At night these exhausted workers went home to overcrowded slums without sewer systems, the perfect breeding grounds for terrible epidemics of cholera, typhoid, and typhus. The poor or lower-middle-class women who stayed at home were without modern appliances or refrigeration. Life as a model housekeeper for those with no servants was constant drudgery.

Problems confronted even better-off women, who were able to turn domestic tasks over to free or slave blacks or immigrant girl servants. The fashions of the day alone were enough to make them inactive and unhealthy, weighted down as they were by multiple petticoats, layers of skirts, and harshly constricting corsets.

They suffered from new illnesses—with symptoms like fainting and hysteria—called "the female malady"—or exhaustion and even invalidism. The physicians who still followed Galen, now called "allopaths" or "Regulars," pampered and medicated women for fat fees. They ordered their "delicate" patients to bed, where they grew even more feeble from the laxatives, enemas, and vomit-inducing drugs of the day. Some of them became addicted to the opiates contained in many of their prescribed "tonics" and sedatives.

Throughout the nineteenth century, few people admired doctors. For one thing, almost anyone could purchase the right to practice medicine simply by enrolling in a few classes or fulfilling a brief apprenticeship. An even more convincing reason for disregard, the harsh therapies of the allopaths seemed to make many sick people worse. Dr. Oliver Wendell Holmes, Sr., father of the famous Supreme Court justice, stated that it would benefit human beings and bring harm only to the fish if the harsh medicines of the Regulars were cast into the ocean. (He called the Irregulars, practitioners who used herbs and gentle nursing, the "nature-trusting heresy.")[3]

Aware of these problems, some women took the advice of the Cult of Domesticity seriously and extended it to its logical conclusion. If women were "morally superior," they reasoned, then they must help solve the social problems of the day—poverty, drunkenness, illiteracy, rundown prisons, slavery, prostitution. Above all, if they were supposed to be guardians of family health, then they would have to be health reformers!

Alternative medical theories were born, and old ones were revived. Most of the so-called Irregular sects emphasized disease prevention through exercise and better nutrition, as well as gentler methods for caring for the ill. Hydropathists used water cures in the form of baths and massive drinking; Thomasonians used gentle herbal cures; homeopaths concentrated on strengthening the patient's ability to fight off disease. Eclectics borrowed from all the sects, using whatever methods seemed useful for a particular patient.

Led by Thomasonian female practitioners, ladies physiological societies were formed for the purpose of sharing health information. As the popularity of the Irregulars grew, the allopaths saw their patients and power slipping away, and quickly launched an all-out war.

Only four medical schools existed in the United States in 1800, and medical education consisted of a mere two or three courses lasting a few months each. Yet, the allopaths considered themselves the only legitimate doctors in the nation. Labeling the Irregulars quacks and charlatans, by 1830 they had used their influence in the state legislatures to push through licensing laws in thirteen states that banned all other medical practitioners.

Their efforts produced a ground swell of opposition. A national campaign was launched to protest the exclusion of the Irregulars. Licensing laws were repealed, and the Irregulars obtained charters to open their own medical schools. Several accepted female students. Between 1840 and 1850 alone, they awarded 11,828 medical degrees.[4]

Encouraged by this victory, other middle-class reformers took heart. The Female Labor Reform Association demanded and won reductions in the intolerable 80- and 90-hour work weeks for women workers in the textile mills.[5]

Realizing that a small but well-organized minority of people could bring about important changes, reformers turned up everywhere, protesting, rallying, lobbying. Dorothea Dix gained fame for her work to improve conditions in poorhouses, insane asylums, and prisons. There were even some daring women who protested against the double standard in sexual behavior and the victimization of prostitutes.

Women who struggled for full equality were isolated

at first from the other reformers. They became the targets of gossip and ridicule by many women and most men.

The struggle against the cruel institution of slavery soon attracted the largest number of reformers, both women and men. They were called "abolitionists." One, Angelina Grimke, a southern white woman, connecting the issue of black slavery and women's rights, angrily orated:

> Let us all first wake up the nation to lift millions of slaves of both sexes from the dust, and turn them into [free] men and then . . . it will be an easy matter to take millions of females from their knees and set them on their feet, or in other words transform them from babies into women.[6]

By 1837 women made up more than half the membership of the abolitionists' antislavery societies. Even so, some abolitionist men argued that the sex equality issue would drive most men away from the antislavery cause. In 1840, at a World Antislavery Society Convention in London, the leaders voted to bar women. After sharp protest from the ranks, they agreed to allow women to observe the proceedings from a curtained-off enclosure. As the conference opened, the excluded women and a few male supporters marched into the gallery, sat down and refused to budge.[7]

After the conference, several angry women made plans for the first recorded women's-rights convention in history. In 1848, at Seneca Falls, New York, three hundred people met to list their grievances and call for voting rights and full equality for both sexes. Their Declaration of Principles pointed out that men monopolized "nearly all profitable employments."[8] The Seneca Falls event inspired similar meetings in other states.

Among the demands of these early feminists was a call for the training of female physicians.[9] The Irregulars' schools had neither money nor space to meet the expanding demand for good health-care providers. The situation seemed so hopeless that some aspiring woman practitioners were urged by friends to disguise themselves as men in order to attend medical colleges.

There is no record of any woman in the United States taking that advice, but in Canada, one brave young woman, Miranda Barry, did just that and managed to evade discovery until her death! Dr. "James" Miranda Barry, born in England in 1797, dressed herself in boy's clothes and attended prestigious Edinburgh University, graduating in 1812 at the age of fifteen. She never shed her male disguise. Joining the British Army, "he" earned a reputation as a superior marksman, swordsman, and surgeon. Serving in India, Jamaica, and many other far-flung British colonies, Dr. Barry fought in many battles.

Short and slim, with a high voice, Barry responded with a quick temper when teased by male colleagues. Despite her precarious position, she stepped into the limelight often, protesting conditions in health facilities and jails. In 1857, she was posted to Canada as Inspector-General of Hospitals, a very high-ranking military office. Perhaps flaunting her amazing trick against the male establishment, she traveled about Canada in a shiny red sleigh, swaddled in luxurious furs and accompanied by a tall black servant, a uniformed footman, and a coachman.

Dr. Barry died at sixty-eight, refusing (for obvious reasons) any medical attention. When an autopsy was performed, the truth was discovered. The army tried but failed to keep the scandal a secret. When the truth leaked out, some were shocked, and others were delighted.[10]

Like Dr. Barry, there were women in the United States who longed for a medical education. In 1849, an eclectic medical school, Central College of New York, admitted Lydia Folger Fowler (1822–1879) and two other women. Soon after Fowler graduated, the college was forced by sinking finances to close its doors. In 1850, Fowler became the first woman professor of medicine at Rochester College, another eclectic institution, and then practiced medicine in New York City for eleven years.[11]

Harriot Hunt (1805–1875) was the first woman to hammer at the doors of prestigious Harvard University. Hunt became interested in medicine when her younger sister Sarah became ill and the attending physicians seemed unable to help her with her "disease of the heart." When the therapies of a Thomasonian husband-wife medical team, Dr. and Mrs. Richard Mott, restored Sarah's health, the two sisters decided to accept the Motts' offer of apprenticeships.

In 1835, the Hunt sisters started their own practice in Boston. Hounded mercilessly by the Regulars of that city, they stopped making house calls and restricted their practice to women and children. In 1847, Harriot Hunt applied for permission to attend lectures without credit at Harvard University. The dean, who happened to be Oliver Wendell Holmes, Sr., agreed, but the students submitted resolutions to the faculty that led to denial of Hunt's modest request. They resolved that

> . . . *no woman of true delicacy would be willing in the presence of men to listen to the discussions of subjects that necessarily come under the consideration of a student of medicine . . . we object to having the company of any female forced upon us who is disposed to unsex herself and to sacrifice her modesty . . .*[12]

Elizabeth Blackwell, born in England in 1821, was the first woman to attend a Regular college. Actually, Blackwell's admission to Geneva Medical College in New York in 1847 was a freak accident. Attracted to medicine after several years of teaching, Blackwell was working for a Quaker doctor who wrote her a strong letter of recommendation for dozens of medical schools. Most of the schools did not even bother to respond. The board of directors of Geneva College, however, received generous donations from Quakers. They did not want to offend Blackwell's sponsor, but neither did they want a woman student.

Certain that the sons of farmers and tradesmen in their student body would overwhelmingly oppose Blackwell's admission, they took the issue to a vote. They announced that Blackwell would not be permitted to attend unless the vote was unanimous. To the dismay of the dean, unlike the privileged students at Harvard, the young men at Geneva handed him their "yes" vote along with a printed statement that ". . . one of the radical principles of a Republican Government is the universal education of both sexes . . ." They also pledged that "no conduct of ours shall cause her to regret her attendance at this institution."[13]

Thus, one year before the Seneca Falls convention, an all-male student body had voted for equal rights, at least for Elizabeth Blackwell! In January 1849, Elizabeth Blackwell graduated with the highest grades in her class.

Hearing about Blackwell's victory, Harriot Hunt once again applied to Harvard. She enclosed a newspaper editorial on Blackwell's admission to Geneva. Harvard finally agreed, but Hunt never set foot in a classroom. Three black men had applied at the same time and were also accepted. When the word spread, the snobbish students immediately rioted against the presence of all four, charging that the "socially repulsive" blacks would lower the value of their credentials and that Hunt should be barred yet again "to preserve the dignity of the school."[14] Harvard did not open its doors to women medical students until nearly a hundred years later (1945); meanwhile several other women had applied and were rebuffed.

Hunt had never been involved with reform movements, but Harvard's rejection pushed her to attend a

In 1849 Elizabeth Blackwell was the first woman
permitted to receive a medical degree in the United
States. She is shown as a medical student attending a
class in an operating room. The inset is a drawing
of the New York Infirmary, which was
founded by Dr. Elizabeth Blackwell.

woman's-rights convention in Worcester, Massachusetts, in 1850. She continued to build her medical practice without the benefit of a license. She was described by friends as a happy woman, although she freely admitted her bitterness over Harvard's rejection.

After this handful of pioneers managed to break into the all-male world of medicine, the doors shut quickly behind them. Over the next decade, only a trickle of women were admitted to allopathic colleges. Even these few graduates found it almost impossible to obtain hands-on clinical experience.

Physicians offered a variety of explanations for rejecting female applicants. Women were too delicate, they said, to endure the fatigue and mental stress of medicine. Others claimed that male patients would be embarrassed. They conveniently forgot about the gynecological examinations performed on immobilized female patients by male doctors. An early graduate later reported that one doctor told her that all of her classmates and the medical staff would think "that only my desire to gratify sexual curiosity would allow me or any woman to take charge of a male ward."[15] When Elizabeth Blackwell went into practice, one newspaper columnist observed, "It is impossible that a woman whose hands reek with gore can be possessed of the same nature or feelings as the generality of women."[16]

In the face of these deep prejudices, an idea gained ground among some equal-rights advocates and women physicians. If the almost all-male colleges and hospitals would not change their policies, they reasoned, women would have to organize their own institutions. All that was required for a medical school charter was a lecture room, four faculty members, a dissecting room, a small front office, and supplies.

The first unchartered medical college for women in the world, the New England Female Medical College, was started in 1848, by a man, Samuel Gregory. His motives were quite different from those of the women.

Gregory had no medical training, but he had written a best-seller on the dangers of sexual appetite, and he used the royalties to finance the school. His interest in training women physicians and midwives came from his prudery, not any desire to elevate women's rights. He believed that male midwifery was an offense to the purity of women.

Marie Zakrzewska (1829–1902), a German midwife called "Zak" by everyone, was the leading faculty member at the college. The Blackwell sisters had encouraged her to study for a medical degree at Western Reserve University in Cleveland, Ohio. Emily Blackwell had graduated from the school in 1854. Both sisters helped to prepare Zakrzewska, and she was admitted to Western Reserve and graduated in 1856. After a dispute with Gregory, Zak left his school and founded the New England Hospital for Women and Children—owned and operated by women.[17]

Gregory's school was plagued with internal warfare, boycotts by male physicians, and financial problems. Although it advertised as a medical college, most of the courses concentrated on midwifery, especially after Zakrzewska's departure. Graduates of the school seldom had learned enough to open their own offices. Some performed volunteer work among the poor or assisted male physicians. One black woman graduate, Rebecca Lee, who most probably would not have found any other place to study, practiced in post-Civil War Richmond, Virginia. When Gregory died in 1872, his New England Female Medical College closed.[18]

In 1842, Ann Preston (1813–1872) contacted a group of Quaker physicians who were frustrated with their efforts to find colleges willing to accept their female apprentices. They discussed Preston's idea of opening a Regular medical school exclusively for women. Like Elizabeth Blackwell, Preston had been rejected by several medical schools after serving a two-year apprenticeship with a Quaker doctor. Eight years later their dream came true when the Female Medical College of Pennsylvania opened its doors as the first chartered medical school for women. The state medical society promptly resolved to expel any member who taught at the new school or helped the faculty in any way.

Despite this, six male physicians taught the first class of forty women. Closed briefly during the Civil War, the college reopened as the Women's Medical College of Philadelphia. In 1970, after one hundred and twenty years as a women's institution, it opened its doors to men and was renamed the Medical College of Pennsylvania.[19]

The success of the Philadelphia college inspired Elizabeth Blackwell and her sister Emily Blackwell to plan a future hospital run by women where female medical students would gain experience with actual patients. After considerable hardship, the Blackwell sisters managed to earn a good living in New York City treating wealthy Quaker women. Elizabeth opened a clinic in the poor ghetto of the Lower East Side. By 1854 the clinic had grown into the Dispensary for Poor Women and Children. With her sister Emily and with Zak coming down from Boston to help raise funds, she created one of the first women's hospitals in the world, the New York Infirmary for Women and Children, in Greenwich Village. Elizabeth Blackwell was told not to make a speech at the opening ceremonies, May 1, 1857. The wealthy donors feared she would speak "like a woman's rights woman."[20]

On two occasions, mobs armed with pickaxes and shovels tried to break down the door, shouting that the female physicians were killing women. According to Zak, the police calmed down the crowd by telling them that they "knew the doctors in that hospital treated the patients in the best possible way, and that no doctor could keep everybody from dying sometime."[21]

In 1868, the Blackwell sisters opened a medical school at the New York Infirmary with much stricter requirements and longer courses than was customary in the male-run schools.[22] Hundreds of women who could not

Dr. Elizabeth Blackwell in later life. She opened the Women's Medical College in 1868 at the New York Infirmary for Women and Children, where women could study to become doctors.

otherwise have become doctors achieved their goals because of the existence of the all-female institutions.

Mary Putnam Jacobi (1842–1906) was one such beneficiary. Her father, George Palmer Putnam, the prestigious publisher of famous American authors such as Nathaniel Hawthorne, Edgar Allan Poe, and James Fenimore Cooper, wanted her to be a writer, but her real interest was science.

After graduating from the Female Medical College of Philadelphia in 1864, Mary interned at Zakrzewska's New England Hospital for Women and Children. Still believing herself ignorant, she yearned to study in Paris at the Ecole de Medicine. Elizabeth Blackwell warned her that the prestigious French school would never admit a woman, but Mary stubbornly traveled there anyway in 1866.

It took her five years of persistence to accomplish her goal. Friends suggested that she put on a male disguise, but she refused. First she was granted permission to join the other students on hospital rounds, keeping silent and keeping her distance. Finally, she was allowed to attend a course, without credit. After auditing all of the required courses, Jacobi finally persuaded the faculty to allow her to take the examination for her medical degree. Her scores were so high that she was allowed to graduate in 1871.

When Jacobi returned home, she joined the faculty at the Woman's Medical College of the Blackwells' New York Infirmary. For the rest of her years, she pounded at the doors of medical societies. In 1880, she was granted membership in the New York Academy of Medicine and taught at the Post Graduate Medical School of New York. At a memorial meeting after her death in 1906, she was paid high honors by the prominent physicians who attended.[23]

Although the pioneer medical women often helped one another, they also had many differences. The Blackwells, Zakrzewska, Jacobi, and others believed there could be no equality for women in medicine until prestigious male allopathic institutions accepted them. Some female physicians believed that true equality would never be achieved until all women were liberated. There was (and still is) often a lurking fear that men would perceive women struggling for equality as "enemies of men."

Perhaps for that reason, Elizabeth Blackwell disassociated herself from the feminist movement and later joined with male doctors to outlaw midwifery. Turning down an invitation to participate in a women's rights convention in Worcester, Massachusetts in 1851, Blackwell stated, "I cannot sympathize fully with an anti-man movement. I have had too much kindness, aid, and just recognition from men."[24]

Dr. Clemence Sophia Lozier disagreed with Blackwell on all counts. She wanted no part of allopathic schools, male- or female-run. Like Harriot Hunt, Lozier became disillusioned with the allopaths when her husband became an invalid and five of her children died under their ministrations.

In 1853, at the age of forty, Lozier graduated at the top of her class from the Eclectic Central Medical College in Syracuse, New York and established a large and successful practice. A firm advocate of women's equality, she headed the New York City Suffrage League for many years. In 1863 she founded the New York Medical College and Hospital for Women, the third women's hospital in the country. Although her students had the legal right to attend clinical lectures in state hospitals, few risked it.

Lozier sent her students to one class at Bellevue hospital, accompanied by her close friend Elizabeth Cady Stanton, a prominent women's rights leader. Stanton reported that they were greeted by a mob of

> *a thousand students with shouts of derisive laughter, and . . . during the lecture, were pelted with chewed balls of paper. The professor selected the*

*most offensive subject and disease for the day,
thinking thereby to end the experiment. As we left
the building, the students had formed themselves
into a double line, through which we passed, mid
jeers and groans, coarse jokes and shouts, pelted
with bits of wood and gravel.*[25]

Lozier immediately called for a protest rally addressed by
several prominent men. Public opinion shifted, and at the
next lecture at Bellevue the mayor sent a marshal and a
squad of police to protect the women.[26]

Over the next four decades, nineteen other women's
medical colleges were founded. Their graduates still
found it next to impossible to gain clinical experience.
After the well-bred young men at the Pennsylvania Hospital in Philadelphia attacked women from the Female
Medical College in a fashion similar to that which Stanton's group had experienced, professors from other medical schools and several hospitals voted to oppose any
mixing of the sexes at clinical settings.[27]

As if these abuses weren't enough, many other factors
discouraged women from pursuing careers in medicine.
As standards for medical education rose, tuition costs
escalated. Most families refused to support their daughters' "notions" of becoming doctors. Since women's jobs
paid far less then men's, it was difficult for a young
woman to save enough to pay for her own education.

It also took considerable courage for a woman to defy
society's conventions. Sex roles were clearly defined,
and a woman who insisted on playing a "male" role was
subjected to cruel jokes and social ostracism. Even
women who managed to scale the highest walls were
usually cheated of their rewards.

During the Civil War, doctors were desperately
needed on the battlefields. Dr. Mary Edwards Walker, a
graduate of Syracuse Medical College, the only woman
in her class and a staunch supporter of women's rights,

An anatomy class at the New York Medical College and Hospital for Women founded in 1863 by Dr. Clemence Sophia Lozier. It was the third women's hospital to be established in the United States. Lozier, a pioneer in medicine, was also a supporter of women's equality.

volunteered her services to the Union Army in 1861. Three years later she was commissioned an acting assistant surgeon and a first lieutenant despite the fact that many army medical officers were reluctant to entrust "the lives of sick and wounded men to such a medical monstrosity."[28]

Walker was captured by the Confederates and imprisoned for four months. Eventually she was traded for a Confederate surgeon. Abraham Lincoln recommended her for the Congressional Medal of Honor, and President Andrew Johnson presented it to her on November 11, 1865. Walker remains the only woman in history to have received that distinguished award.

In 1917, two years before Walker's death, the Army ruled that only a man carrying a weapon and engaged in active combat could receive the Medal of Honor. It asked Walker to return hers. She refused, despite harassment and ridicule, even by her own family. Two year later, she died at age 87, penniless and alone. In 1977, a revived feminist movement brought the issue before Congress, and Mary Walker's medal was officially restored to her posthumously.[29]

After the Civil War, the freeing of the slaves encouraged women to push harder for their own freedom. Dr. Mary Putnam Jacobi convinced wealthy women in the Boston area to raise money for women's scholarships to the most prestigious male medical schools. In 1865, finding no school willing to accept the idea, the donors turned the money over to the Blackwells' hospital instead.

It seemed that the women "separatists" were winning the debate by default.[30] Pound as hard as women like the Blackwells might, they found the male establishment still reluctant to open the doors to equality between the sexes.

four

OPENING THE DOORS AT LAST

Another disease has become epidemic, 'The woman question' in relation to medicine is only one of the forms in which the *pestis muliebris* vexes the world. In other shapes it attacks the bar, wriggles into the jury box, and clearly means to mount upon the bench . . . it raves at political meetings, harangues in the lecture-room, infects the masses with its poisons . . . and is of the sort in which Eve's daughters excel.

—Statement by Alfred Stillé in the 1871 *Transactions of the American Medical Association.*[1]

During the short-lived Reconstruction era after the Civil War, the federal government sponsored land-grant colleges for the education of African Americans. These schools, such as the University of Michigan and Syracuse University, also admitted a few women beginning in 1869. By the late 1880s, several private medical colleges also admitted some women. Most women and men, however, still practiced medicine without licenses, learning on their own or apprenticing themselves to "trained" doctors.

Black and Jewish women, seldom among the handful of women accepted by the new coed schools, were grateful for the existence of the less prejudiced Women's Med-

MARTINSON MIDDLE SCHOOL
LIBRARY
Marshfield, Mass. 02050

ical College of Philadelphia. Sarah Cohen May, the daughter of poor Jewish immigrants, graduated in its class of 1879. She established her practice in Philadelphia, serving mainly Eastern European Jews who had fled the murderous persecutions of the Russian Czar in the 1880s. Her Yiddish-speaking working-class patients came to see "Dr. Sarah" when they were ill because she spoke their language and understood their religious customs.[2]

By 1881, four hundred and seventy women in the United States possessed Regular medical degrees. Women's magazines ran stories about the achievements of professional women. Biographical dictionaries of prominent American women appeared, as well as several novels with women physicians as their main characters, like Mark Twain's *The Gilded Age*, published in 1873. The more conservative women's publications, dedicated to Victorian ideals, urged readers to maintain their feminine modesty and patronize doctors of their own sex.[3]

There were no separate women's colleges in Washington D.C., but in the closing decades of the nineteenth century most of the area's medical schools experimented briefly with limited coeducation, with women constituting 3 to 5 percent of entering classes.[4] The schools decided to admit women when their treasuries were low. Later, under one pretext or another, the schools returned to their male-only policies. Georgetown admitted women for only one year. National University, a small underfunded college, allowed a few women to enter each year until 1903.

At Columbian College (later renamed George Washington University) a scandal rocked Washington in the spring of 1892, when a group of women medical students were suddenly expelled by the college and coeducation was scrapped. Rumors spread over the capital, but the college administration refused to reveal its reasons, saying only that coeducation had failed. In her 1924 biography, Dr. Marie Zakrzewska referred vaguely to the incident. Students and professors, she wrote, "made the path of the women students as rough and stoney as possible."[5] Thirty years later, Zakrzewska's biographer claimed that the doctor told her that in the dissecting laboratory, some male students "debased themselves by offering insult, not only to the women medical students, but also to the helpless bodies."[6] The women present in the laboratory were expelled. Within a short time, *all* women were barred from the school.

Deprived of their education, the women petitioned and protested, all to no avail. They solicited statements of support from women's organizations, but did not appeal for help to the women's suffrage groups. Unlike their predecessors, this so-called post-pioneer generation of women had little use for women's-rights activists, in some cases sharing the widespread opinion of the day that suffragists were "manly women." Some even belittled openly the earlier women's movement that had encouraged the female pioneers of medicine. The women believed that the advances they enjoyed were a simple result of normal social progress. The leader of the women students expelled by Columbian College went even further, stating that the movement did more harm than good.

Despite their careful avoidance of any group that could offend the school's decision makers, the Columbian students were not reinstated. Meanwhile, enrollment of white females at Howard and National in the Washington D.C. area increased a little. A few women briefly flirted with the idea of opening a women's college in Washington D.C. But before concrete plans could be made, they heard better news that attracted them to nearby Baltimore.

Scientific discoveries were occurring in Europe's major cities in the 1880s, and medicine was being transformed. Medical therapies changed as new drugs like salicylic acid (aspirin), urine tests, blood tests, and instruments like the stethoscope were introduced. American students who could afford the cost attended German or French universities and returned to the United States as pediatricians, dermatologists, ophthalmologic specialists, and gynecologists. Specialization was becoming the road to wealth. Specialists formed their own societies and began urging standardization of medical training in the United States—tougher entrance requirements, longer courses of study, final exams, strict licensing laws. The latest findings were debated in the pages of newly founded scientific journals. As the public began to accept the new "modern" approaches, the Irregulars feuded among themselves, and their numbers declined.

In 1878, Harvard once again turned down a large donation because it was tied to the acceptance of female students. Wealthy women later raised a half-million dollars and offered it to Johns Hopkins University in Baltimore, Maryland. In 1893, a group of American doctors who had graduated from German medical schools convinced the Johns Hopkins trustees to accept the donation and build a medical school open to women. Many other schools followed, and in a few years, women comprised one-quarter to one-third of the nation's medical school students.[7]

In 1900, Tufts University Medical School in Boston announced that 42 percent of its graduates were women. These "gentle creatures who would faint at the sight of blood" had captured the greater percentage of academic honors.[8] Even state medical societies began to admit women, albeit by ones and twos.

The powerful AMA (American Medical Association), however, could not be convinced to open its steel doors. Nor would it retract its vicious anti-woman articles, like the one quoted at the beginning of this chapter. Women were not admitted into the AMA until 1915, shortly *after* they formed their own Medical Women's National Association. A few prestigious all-male "medical clubs" waited even longer than the AMA. The College of Physicians of Philadelphia did not move to admit women until 1929, and then delayed the event until 1932![9]

By the turn of the century, most women desiring a medical career preferred to attend coed schools. They believed it was no longer necessary to support all-women's medical schools. The Board of Trustees of New York Infirmary announced its decision to close the college in 1899 when Cornell University's medical school accepted women. Emily Blackwell, who had cofounded the New York Infirmary thirty-one years earlier, expressed the majority opinion. "We held open the doors for women until broader gates had swung wide for their admission."[10] There is no record that anyone expressed fears that the male gatekeepers at the "broader gates" might one day padlock them again.

The Women's Medical College of Philadelphia, however, decided to stay in business. Its staff worried that as a minority in men's institutions, women students might be neglected. These separatists believed that women practiced a unique style of medicine, in touch with the patient's need for nurturance. The integrationists disagreed. They believed that the more women physicians patterned themselves after male doctors, the more rapidly they would reach an equal footing with professional men.

By 1903, only three out of seventeen women's colleges still existed. One of them, the Women's Medical College of Baltimore founded in 1882, was a "woman's college" in terms of its student body only. Just one woman had been made a member of the board of trustees after 1892.[11]

It appeared at first that women's decisions to enter coed institutions had been wise. During this so-called Gilded Age, the number of women doctors rose from 2,423 in 1880 to more than 7,000 by 1900! About 75 percent of medical schools became coeducational, with women making up from 25 to nearly 50 percent of enrollments.

In their graduating classes, the women won a higher percentage of academic honors than the men. Furthermore, although male physicians had long said that an education would be wasted on women because they would marry and stop working, 90 percent of female graduates of medical schools were active physicians in 1900.[12]

Most of the Gilded Age female doctors considered themselves "new women." Many rejected the whole idea of marriage in a society where most women lost all legal rights to husbands. As one woman writer expressed it in the *Journal of the Moral Education Society*:

> *A woman . . . who has ambition and energy to develop her powers, will not be satisfied to tie herself down in the soul-cramping marriage . . . a woman's highest duty to herself and humanity demands her full development as a Woman,* not as a *Wife* or a *Mother.*[13]

American medical women leaped ahead of European women. Coed medical schools existed only in Switzerland. The enlightened German universities did not enroll women until 1899, six years after Johns Hopkins opened its doors to women. Women had not developed their own colleges in Europe for fear that graduates might be regarded as second-class doctors.[14]

Mary Putnam Jacobi in an essay on woman in medicine applauded the Johns Hopkins victory as an event that would place "an entire new horizon . . . before us."[15] She could not have been more mistaken!

five

SLAMMED DOORS

Until I took my internship I had never seen a woman operate, and I do not think those of you who have had your training in this school can realize what it means . . . it is almost inevitable, if you never have seen a woman doing anything, to think she cannot do it quite as well as a man . . .

—Dr. Alice Weld Tallant, speaking at an alumni meeting of the Women's Medical College of Philadelphia in 1912.[1]

As women physicians celebrated their remarkable leap forward, a campaign against other women health providers was intensified.

In the early years of the twentieth century, midwives still attended about half of all births. Working mostly among poorer people, American-born and immigrants, midwives delivered babies in tenements and shacks, prairie schooners (covered wagons) and log cabins. In the Southwest, they were called "*curanderas*";[2] in the South they were "Grannys." Most midwives asked for only a few dollars and were willing to help women who could not pay at all. The new obstetricians, who charged high fees, had no intention of "giving away" their services.

As the government grew stronger, state boards of health were opened in many states and began paying fees for doctors' services to the poor. Physicians, who recognized the money to be made in treating the poor, promptly denounced midwives as dirty, drunken, and incompetent. The midwives could scarcely defend themselves, for they had no support from the women doctors or the women's movement, they were isolated from one another, and their patients were powerless. Although studies in the early 1900s showed that infant and maternal death rates were about the same for deliveries by midwives as deliveries by obstetricians, the general public accepted the negative stereotypes circulated by the doctors.

Massachusetts, where factory women depended almost entirely on deliveries at home, was the first state to ban midwifery (1907). Consequently, midwives proceeded to practice illegally, and the number of midwife-attended births actually increased slightly by 1913!

In many states, the issue was fiercely debated. Health reformers, concerned that so many pregnant women and new mothers would be left with no one to turn to, called for training and licensing programs similar to those in England and Europe. Although a few underfunded facilities were set up, midwives, for the most part, were driven out of business by World War II.

Some writers claim that midwives vanished because of attacks by a sexist male medical system. However, since immigrant families were most likely to use midwives, other writers point to the major decline in immigration following the highly restrictive Immigration Act of 1924. (This legislation was passed to limit the militant labor-union organizing by some of the twenty-four million immigrants admitted since 1890.) Still others point to a decline in the birth rate and the growing preference of poor women to give birth in the charity clinics of newly created scientific hospitals doing research and offering "modern" patient care.[3]

Whatever reason most influenced the outcome, until recent years midwives were forgotten health workers, museum pieces from the past. After World War II, only two training schools stayed open, both founded during the depression: the New York Maternity Center Association's school and the Kentucky Frontier Nursing Service's school.[4]

Women doctors seemed completely unaware that once midwives were out of the way, they themselves could become the next targets. It did not dawn on them that the first step they had taken toward equality was to be their last for three-quarters of the twentieth century!

Signs of the change became clear early. At the University of Michigan Medical School during the school year of 1893, almost 19 percent of the students were women, but fourteen years later, the numbers had slipped to less than 6 percent. Johns Hopkins University, where Dr. Jacobi's "new horizon" had started, underwent the same kind of startling change.[5] And these were not temporary setbacks. Until the 1970s, only 7 percent or less of the physicians in the United States were female.[6]

Strangely, this decline was strictly an American phenomenon. Although it took longer for Europe's medical schools to open to women, once they did, they remained open. As the century progressed, most countries had at least 20 percent women physicians. Finland, the Philippines, and Thailand had more than 25 percent. In the socialist nations of the Soviet Union and Eastern Europe, the vast majority of doctors were women.[7]

There are many theories to explain this mystery of the "slammed doors." Mary Walsh Roth believes that the hostility of male faculty and students had been hidden only temporarily. As soon as the women's colleges closed their doors and women could study in only a few schools, a full-scale offensive was launched to exclude them again.[8]

Certainly, the women who attended medical college during the Gilded Age had to be aware of the continued hostility of most male students and faculty. For one thing, universities that continued to exclude women were considered far more prestigious than coed schools. As late as 1962, historian Frederick Rudolph applauded male colleges like Yale, Princeton, and Harvard for preserving "the liberal inheritance of Western Civilization in the United States by protecting it from the debilitating, feminizing, corrupting influences which shaped its career where coeducation prevailed."[9] Women apparently had hoped that as their ranks swelled, the male hostility would diminish.

At many liberal arts coeducational colleges in the late 1880s, a strange kind of tracking system began to affect female undergraduates. A new major, "home management education," reminiscent of the Cult of Domesticity, was introduced. Women were urged to major in this field. These "scientific" home economics programs included classes with titles such as Sanitary Chemistry, Food Principles, and Home Sanitation.[10] They were thinly disguised cooking, cleaning, and hygiene courses, designed to elevate the status of motherhood and housewifery.

There were voices of opposition to this charade. A New York Times article called it "a widespread movement . . . to raise the standard of menial domestic duties by honoring them with the title of science."[11]

Within a few decades, 240 colleges had established degree programs in home economics or domestic science. Women of the poorer classes, particularly recent immigrants, were offered scholarships to enroll in these courses of study. Most of the more prestigious women's colleges did not join the movement, but as the pendulum swung back to an idealization of housekeeping roles for women, more of their graduates were marrying. By 1910, fewer continued on to graduate school.

Some writers blame this subtle propaganda war for the decreasing numbers of women in medical school. The home management movement had an impact on many women, but it seems unlikely that it was the cause of the precipitous decline in the number of women physicians. In 1893, as thousands of wide-eyed visitors admired a scientific kitchen exhibit at the Chicago World's Fair, hundreds of middle- and upper-class women were moving into coed universities to study medicine.

Fear of competition seems a more likely culprit. The author of an article in the *Journal of the American Medical Association* in 1895 expressed the hope that the new home economics programs for women would end the "competition of labor between the sexes"[12] These words reflected the concerns of many male physicians who had at first believed that only a tiny group of "unfeminine" women would be interested in a career in medicine. These doctors were seeing many more women entering medicine than anticipated. In 1870 there were 55,000 trained doctors. The 1900 Census reported almost 120,000 doctors, and their ranks were growing many times faster than the rate of population growth. Given the increasing number of doctors entering the field, the increase in the number of women doctors was especially resented. As early as 1898, the elite physicians were complaining bitterly that because of women crowding into their profession, they were failing financially, even to "the starving point," as one editorial in the AMA's journal complained.[13]

Because fair competition between all applicants often increased the percentage of female students, many colleges initiated secret quota systems. Unknowingly, women competed against one another for a sharply reduced number of openings and were rejected when those slots were filled. Without access to policy-making bodies, applicants could fuss and fume but prove nothing. Women were once again bloodying their fists pounding against steel doors.

Many researchers blame "professionalization" for the sudden reversal of policy. Professionalization of medicine usually refers to the standardization of therapies and the creation of institutions to safeguard those standards through carefully policed licensing. Others consider professionalization a minor cause, pointing to the fact that *the greatest gains for women were made in the late nineteenth century, a period of rapid professionalization.*

The lack of participation in policy-making bodies is surely a key clue for the solution of the mystery. It is true that women had been admitted to medical schools *as students* in fairly large numbers, but they had almost never been hired as administrators or faculty members. Those in the *decision-making* seats had the power to reverse women's victories.

In the 1970s, Mary Roth Walsh studied the histories of Tufts Medical School and Boston University and found out more about this clue. When Tufts opened as a coed school in 1893, students were selected according to their scores on admissions exams. In 1900, two-fifths of the graduating class was female. In 1906, all five seniors elected to the Phi Beta Kappa Society for highest academic achievement were women. And by the following year, only one-third of the freshman class was male.

The newly appointed college president, Rev. Dr. Frederick W. Hamilton, claimed that the men were doing poorly on admissions tests or in the classrooms because they were intimidated by the presence of women.[14] The administration decided to open a separate women's college, Jackson, *without a medical school of its own.* In 1910, at the inauguration of Jackson College, male students at Tufts lit bonfires, tooted on horns, and paddled some of the women. By 1919, most women applicants to Tufts had been shunted over to Jackson. Tufts Medical School graduated only two women out of one hundred students that year. Elsewhere in the nation similar tactics were used to reverse coed policies and put women "back in their place." Nationally, female enrollment in medical school dropped by one-third from 1895 to 1903.[15]

Even homeopathic schools like Boston University, always a welcome haven for women students, joined the backlash parade. When there had been almost no openings in Regular schools, women had kept the homeopathic colleges alive with their tuition payments. The Boston University class of 1886, for example, was 56 percent female. In 1918, the college changed its medical curriculum in order to compete with the allopathic schools. Over the next twenty years, the proportion of women students shrank to less than 10 percent. By 1939, *there was not a single woman in the graduating class!*

Still dissatisfied with the status and income of their all-male membership, the AMA embarked on a program to complete the standardization of the medical profession. Perhaps the AMA leaders hoped that if fewer medical schools existed and if curricula at those schools were made more difficult and tuition raised, they could eliminate Irregulars and women from the ranks of medicine.

By the turn of the century, new millionaire families had created philanthropic foundations. The Carnegie Foundation hired Abraham Flexner, a man with no medical experience, to judge the quality of medical schools. Flexner visited 155 institutions, briefly examining student credentials to determine the quality of each school.

Most states had by then set new legal standards for accreditation of their medical schools. Independent bodies examined each university and reported on its qualities. Anything less than a "grade A" meant fewer donations from wealthy contributors, which in turn meant less equipment, lower salaries for teachers, and an even lower grade the next time.

Among Flexner's targets were not only many inferior "diploma mills" but also the surviving medical schools for women. Flexner decided that women's medical colleges had no reason for existing. He incorrectly claimed that medical schools in the United States and Canada were "open to women upon practically the same terms as men."[16] (Apparently, Mr. Flexner had not heard the news about the precipitous drop in women's enrollments at medical colleges.)

In 1910 the Carnegie Foundation published the results: *Medical Education in the United States and Canada.*[17] The so-called Flexner Report was sharply critical of almost every medical school in the country. Johns Hopkins was held up as the model. Flexner recommended strict premedical school educational requirements, longer courses of study, stiff clinical requirements, and the affiliation of medical schools with hospitals and clinics. He was put in charge of administering over $300 million donated by the Rockefeller and Carnegie Foundations for medical education and research. Thus, money went only to the schools he approved.

By 1920, only 85 of the 155 medical schools originally assessed by Flexner remained open. Of the three medical schools for women that had survived into the twentieth century, two closed in the next few years, knowing that grants and donations would shrink as a result of Flexner's false claims and his control of the purse strings. As the colleges that had welcomed women disappeared, those endowed by the foundations no longer needed the women's tuition fees; thus the number of slots for women narrowed even more.

The cost of a medical education escalated to meet Flexner's new requirements. Many working- and middle-class men had to abandon their dreams too. Working women, who earned far less than men, did not have any resources to study medicine. Parents were far less likely to sacrifice for a daughter's education than for a son's.

Even if the money could be scraped together, it took courage to oppose the prevailing opinion that women should be satisfied with the role of wife, mother, and "scientific" housekeeper. To face mockery and then to be rejected by one college after the other was embarrassing and discouraging. Many women accepted defeat and turned to nursing—an expanding although underpaid field for women only (see Chapter VII).

By 1929, almost twenty years after the Flexner Report, only 481 women, compared with 13,174 men, applied to schools of medicine. Administrators could easily blame women for the demise of women doctors on the grounds that they had accepted 65.5 percent of female applicants and 51 percent of the males.[18] Surely, they could say, this was perfectly fair!

We may wonder why so many twentieth-century women abandoned the struggle more easily than did the pioneers of medicine of the previous century. Some students of the subject believe that the first female physicians took courage from the early women's rights movements.[19] Many of them had operated on the principle of solidarity that governed the early struggles for workers' rights—united we stand; divided we fall. But women during the Gilded Age and later operated as individuals, each one attempting to improve her own career chances. They competed hopelessly with men and of course with one another for shrinking opportunities.

Except for some tiny groups still struggling for *full* equality for women, by the time of the Flexner Report the larger women's movement was concentrating all its energies on winning the right to vote. The women's-rights movement in Washington, D.C. in the 1880s and 1890s, for example, had only a handful of regular members, three women doctors among them. Ignored by their colleagues, the women doctors failed even to secure appointments for female physicians in women's prisons, almshouses, public hospitals, and a girls' reform school.[20]

In 1915 a small group of women doctors formed the National Women's Medical Association to assist women professionals. Renamed the American Medical Women's Association (AMWA) in 1919, members were urged to join the American Medical Association when it accepted women. They tried to make it clear that they were not separatists but that they needed an organization of their own to attempt to stem the mounting tide against women.

Two-thirds of the women doctors in the United States declined to join the AMWA. A few even circulated petitions against it. The women continued their individual struggles for acceptance by the male-governed medical associations, clinics, and hospitals. Even the few who won admission to these learned bodies remained isolated bystanders, unable to influence policy.

One woman doctor commented that before admission to the AMA, "Women doctors were on the outside standing together. Now they were on the inside sitting alone."[21]

The only powerful women's group, the National American Womens Suffrage Association (NAWSA), believed that if political equality was won at the voting polls the other inequalities could be combated more easily. In 1913, they intensified their struggle for a Nineteenth Amendment to the Constitution, guaranteeing suffrage to women. This was exactly when the decline of women in the professions was most noticeable.

The Fifteenth Amendment had guaranteed black *men* the right to vote, but in the South, they were stopped by poll taxes, difficult literacy tests, and fear of attack by the rising numbers of Ku Klux Klan night riders. Mob lynchings had increased to alarming proportions. Repeal of the Fifteenth Amendment was a distinct possibility.

The southern states had no intention of allowing black *women* to vote, and they wanted to be able to set their own laws on the question. Consequently the southern-based Woman Suffrage Conference wanted women's suffrage on a state-by-state basis. Bending to these sectional pressures, the national suffrage movement reaffirmed states' rights and agreed to water down its demands. Debate on the subject raged through the women's movement, dividing its ranks.[22]

These vital issues, as well as an international anti-lynching movement led by Ida B. Wells, a black journalist from Memphis, consumed the time and passions of the most active women's-rights advocates. When thousands

Women in academic robes march down Fifth Avenue in New York City, about 1910, to promote women's right to vote. The movement for women's equality was an indispensable aid to the women struggling for equality in the medical profession.

of women marched up Pennsylvania Avenue past Woodrow Wilson's White House in 1917 demanding the vote, they were attacked by white men. Arrested and jailed, they went on highly publicized hunger strikes. Black and white women alike were far too busy to pay attention to the disappearance of the women doctors.

Even in 1918, when the Anthony amendment—named after the leader Susan B. Anthony—granting women the right to vote had finally passed through both houses of Congress, the battle for state ratification became the main work of the women's movement. When victory came, the exhausted women's movement mistakenly expected significant changes to result.

Meanwhile, medical coeducation had been all but extinguished. Medical classes were limited to 5 or 6 percent women.[23] During World War I, the situation briefly improved. When thousands of young men went off to fight on the battlefields of Europe in 1917, universities worried about their depleted tuition income. Thirteen medical schools including Columbia, Yale, and Harvard agreed to admit women and slowly began planning for this long-delayed event.

With fewer young men applying for internships, some hospitals quietly obtained the names of leading woman medical students and asked them to apply. Massachusetts General Hospital appointed its first woman intern, Dr. Mary Wright, to serve in their pediatrics division in 1919, but its reluctance to do so was recorded: The choice had been between one of two "undesirable male Hebrews" [Jews] or a woman![24]

Despite a desperate need for surgeons on the war front, women surgeons were allowed to serve only on a contract basis. Paid by the hour without the military commissions given to male surgeons, they earned less and were deprived of retirement income and other benefits.

The AMWA urged their members to accept the insulting conditions and support the war effort, just as black doctors were doing despite the Army's segregationist policies. Fifty-five women doctors volunteered, working near battle lines to stitch together horribly wounded young soldiers. As one such surgeon sarcastically told a congressional committee on the eve of World War II, the women doctors did have one military benefit. When they died they could be buried in Arlington Cemetery.[25]

Rebelling against this obvious inequality, a handful of American women physicians went to Europe and volunteered to serve in the French army. They were accepted gratefully and later were awarded the French medal of honor (croix de guerre) for their service under fire.[26]

Meanwhile, a new brick door had been erected in most states. Before anyone could be licensed to practice medicine they were required by the state to serve an internship and residency at a hospital. The problem was that in the 1890s only six hospitals—all of them women's hospitals—had regularly appointed female interns. Now, with most of the women's institutions long gone, a mere trickle of women managed to land internships—and those in less desirable hospitals. Male graduates had a good chance to land an internship near family and friends, but women had to take what they could get, often moving to remote areas far from loved ones. Even then, they were usually the *only* woman intern on the premises, isolated and with no network to turn to for help.

When World War I ended, Harvard quickly canceled the plan it had not yet carried out to admit a few women. Internships for women became even scarcer and were required in *more* states. A measly 8 percent of hospitals and clinics were willing to train a few women in 1921.[27] Even maternity hospitals refused to accept female interns. When the AMWA complained, it was told separate housing facilities for women were not available. The AMWA countered that the hospitals managed to house nurses, matrons, and female patients.

Naturally, it seemed futile to study medicine if it was impossible to complete the required postgraduate clinical work. Young high school and college women rarely even considered the possibility of medicine as their career. Moreover, once the women's medical schools closed, there were almost no role models. Very few people ever *saw* a woman doctor or were told that they existed. Even in women's hospitals, interns, doctors, and administrators were almost always male.

Medical school teaching opportunities also were almost nonexistent. In 1899, when Cornell University opened its medical school to women and the women's New York infirmary decided to close, Emily Blackwell expressed her sorrow about the female teachers at the Infirmary who lost their jobs. Thirteen years later there was not even one woman instructor at Cornell Medical School or its clinical services.

A few prestigious women joined faculties here and there. Almost always they were the sole woman professor on the faculty and were deprived of the promotions given to male colleagues. In 1919, Harvard hired Dr. Alice Hamilton as an assistant professor at the medical school. A renowned expert in the new field of industrial medicine, Hamilton retired in 1933, still an assistant professor.

Many women accepted their subordinate roles, having learned them in early childhood. In many ways this pattern has endured right up to the present. Little girls are told to be "feminine." Miniature stoves, ironing boards, dolls, baby carriages, and nurse sets are traditionally "girls' toys." Boys are offered war toys, chemistry sets, and doctors' kits.

Some scholars now believe that these environmental and psychological factors are important reasons why women did not push harder in the twentieth century to enter medicine and other professions.[29] Without role models, without support networks, with many people mocking their efforts and questioning their "femininity," with financial worries and institutional rejection, women considering a medical career faced untold anxiety.

Again, another world war temporarily helped those who had, despite all the pressures, become doctors. By the time the United States entered World War II in December 1941, only about 5 percent of graduating medical students were women. Even for these few women, there were still not enough internships, although there was a surplus for male applicants.

The need for medical personnel during the Second World War was desperate. A well-publicized AMWA survey demonstrated that many women doctors were anxious to serve. Public Law 252 was passed on September 23, 1941, authorizing President Franklin Delano Roosevelt to make temporary appointments of "qualified persons" as officers in the United States Army. Women quickly learned that the word "persons" meant white males. Again, they were offered posts as uncommissioned contract surgeons.

The following year, they were offered a chance to become doctors in the Women's Army Auxiliary Corps (WAACS), away from the military zones where doctors were urgently needed. Some accepted the offer, but once again nine women went abroad and joined the British Medical Corps.[30]

As the war dragged on and the need for front-line physicians escalated, under AMWA pressure Congress passed legislation permitting women to serve in the Army and Navy medical corps. For their part, to meet the shortage of doctors the medical schools enlarged their freshman classes. The government paid the tuition for large numbers of young men, but even though women were being accepted as students they had to pay their own way. By 1945, the last year of the war, over 14 percent of the freshman students in medical schools were female, an almost threefold increase.[31]

Harvard University had steadfastly maintained its two-century ban on women. By the beginning of World War II, women didn't even bother to apply, knowing they

*Members of the Women's Army Corps sail
for Europe during World War II. Women doctors joined
the Women's Army Auxiliary Corps although they were
not assigned to the front lines.*

would receive a standard form rejection letter known as "Letter to Ladies." In 1943, a rumor spread that Harvard's enrollments were down and women would be admitted after all. Applications poured in. The 1945 freshman class included twelve women. The number of hospitals accepting women interns also increased as male applications declined.[32] Once more optimism spread that medicine would be opening up to women.

Within a year after the end of the war, women were no longer welcomed. Those who had worked in the war industries—the much-celebrated Rosie the Riveters—were sent home permanently. Likewise, women doctors were removed from their posts or delegated to routine jobs. The medical schools once again imposed their secret quotas.[33] By 1955, a new low point had been reached. Many schools that had welcomed women during the war no longer had a single female student.

Now that women were no longer needed, polls were published to justify the sudden change. In 1949 and 1957, hospital chiefs of staff and male physicians gave familiar answers to questionnaires asking them their opinions of female doctors. Many of them commented that women doctors were "emotionally unstable," "talk too much," and "get pregnant"! One dean actually declared that he preferred a third-rate man to a first-rate woman doctor.[34]

Despite this rampant gender discrimination, there were always exceptional women who not only managed to become physicians but performed so outstandingly that they could not be ignored. Among them was Dr. Florence Sabin, whose discoveries on the lymphatic system had a dramatic impact on medicine. In 1925 she became the first woman to become a full member of the staff of the Rockefeller Institute and the first to be elected to the National Academy of Sciences. Louise Pearce led a Rockefeller Institute research group to the Congo to study sleeping sickness. Hellen Taussig, along with Dr. Alfred

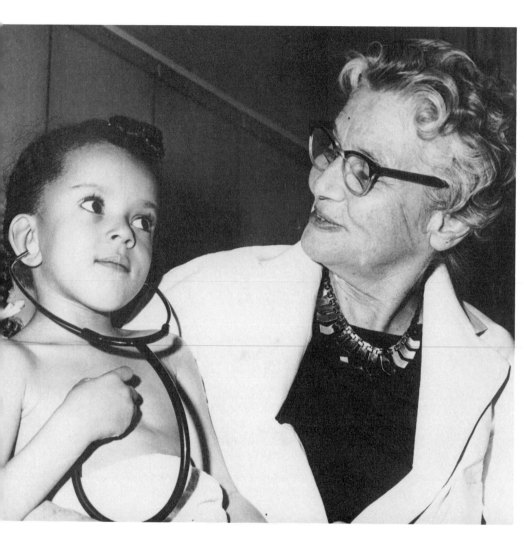

In 1945, Dr. Helen Taussig, along with Dr. Alfred Blalock,
developed the heart operation that saves the lives of "blue
babies." Dr. Blalock was elected to the National
Academy of Science, but not his female coauthor, Dr.
Taussig. Dr. Taussig had refused to join the American
Medical Association because of its stand against Medicare.
The little girl at left was born with her heart slightly on
the right side of the body, instead of the normal left.

Blalock, codeveloped the operation for blue babies, a giant step in modern heart surgery. In 1945 when the two doctors published the results of their operations, Dr. Blalock was elected to the National Academy of Science, an honor never extended to his female coauthor, Dr. Taussig.

Only two women physicians were ever invited to serve at the White House: Dr. Anna Easton Lake, by President Grover Cleveland[35] and Dr. Janet Travell by President John F. Kennedy.[36]

Dr. Marjorie Horning has received medals for her work on the transfer of drugs from a pregnant woman to her child. Until her important research, it was believed that the fetus was protected by the placenta. When she began her laboratory work in the 1940s and 1950s, she worked as an *unpaid* aide in the University of Pennsylvania laboratory. Women then were excluded even from paid laboratory jobs.[37]

These exceptional women were often referred to whenever women complained about the handicaps they would suffer if they attempted a medical career. The list is pathetically short compared with the long roll call of women who were kept from realizing their potential in the world of medicine.

In the fall of 1946, as the doors shut again after World War II, a bitter full-page advertisement signed by prominent women doctors appeared in the *New York Herald Tribune*—"DOCTORS WANTED: NO WOMEN NEED APPLY."[38]

six

KNOCKING AT BACK DOORS

Everything to this race is new and strange and inspiring. There is a quickening of its pulse and a glowing of its self-consciousness. Aha, I can rival that! I can aspire to that! I can honor my name and vindicate my race! This . . . is the enthusiasm which stirs the genius of young Africa in America.

—Anna Julia Cooper, Principal of the Colored High School in Washington, D.C., during the Gilded Age.[1]

The story of black women physicians must be told separately. They faced far more discouraging blockades in their paths than those encountered by white women.[2] Even during the Gilded Age, when women like Anna Cooper (quoted above) thought that black women would find new and wonderful opportunities, the glitter quickly proved to be only the dull glint of brass.

During the years before the Civil War, when the courageous women pioneers of medicine were struggling to gain admittance to medical schools and hospitals, the majority of black men and women labored in captivity on southern plantations. Under the savage whip of slavery, they had only one goal—freedom, even if it meant the "freedom" of most northern blacks who worked at the most menial jobs.

A scattering of free African-American men worked as apprentices to a handful of sympathetic white doctors. The most daring of them pounded on the doors and gained admittance by ones and twos to lesser-known medical schools.[3] In 1847, David J. Peck, officially the nation's first black doctor, graduated from Rush Medical College in Chicago. Thirteen years later, only nine schools had admitted one or more black men to their lectures. Many times that number had applied and been turned down.

A few male slaves, like James Derham, were purchased by doctors and learned medical skills. Derham was eventually freed by his master and set up a practice among other free African Americans.

If there were black women doctors before the Civil War years, there are no records of their existence. The *Journal of the American Medical Association* published two articles on African-American physicians during its long history. One was in 1942 and the other in 1969. Neither so much as referred to black women.[4]

It seems possible that some free African-American women, perhaps a few "Granny midwives" or young women who managed to obtain a few years of schooling, dreamed of studying medicine. Perhaps they quickly realized that the dream was next to impossible. They had three strikes against them: the usual sex discrimination against women; the racism of white men and women; and the "competition" of African-American men. In addition, since most of them were uneducated and able to find only low-paying domestic work, they could not afford even low tuition.

Black medicine in America started when African healers were brought to the American colonies on slave ships. The crowded unsanitary vessels were breeding grounds for disease. Often the larger part of a human cargo and its associated profits were wiped out by typhus, diphtheria, or scarlet fever. Realizing the advantages of keeping their captives alive and healthy-looking for the auction block, slave traders included African healers of both genders on their nightmare vessels.

Living in crowded shanties with no sanitation, newly arrived slaves were lucky to stay alive. About one-quarter of them died during their first few months of captivity. Epidemics were frequent and deadly. In Louisiana in 1832 cholera killed over five thousand slaves in a two-week period—a four-million-dollar loss for planters.

When black healers were notably successful in dealing with the health problems of their own people, word quickly spread. The slave Cesar had herbal and root medicines that worked so well that he was taken from his field chores and kept busy curing white people. In 1751, he was granted his freedom by the South Carolina General Assembly with a small annual stipend for his discovery of a rattlesnake-bite remedy.[5]

The names of a few black "doctresses" have been found in plantation property inventories and fugitive slave notices in newspapers. The doctresses served as midwives and herbal medicine women in the slave quarters and sometimes at the master's big house. There was Elsey, on a Georgia plantation; Aggy in Virginia. A slave on an Alabama plantation named Mary had an excellent record for saving lives. When these women were called upon to tend a white person, they must have trembled with fear. Laws called for the death sentence for slaves who prepared medicines "with intent to poison."[6]

By 1776, there were over half a million slaves in the newborn United States. Very few of the white apprentice-trained practitioners or university-educated physicians were willing to tend black people, slave or free. Without medical attention, the health of black people deteriorated even further by 1860, when the slave population had grown to approximately four million.

Slave Granny midwives were especially important on

large plantations. Every new baby born to a slave mother added to the master's wealth. The sheer numbers of women these midwives had birthed in the slave quarters often made them more experienced than the white doctors. Some of the Granny midwives, having gained fame for saving women who might otherwise have died in labor, were summoned to attend at the births of their masters' and mistresses' babies. The wealthiest planters, however, preferred to use white male physicians both as their family doctors and in the slave quarters.

Runaway slaves who eluded their pursuers and managed to reach the North soon found that it did not match the mythology of an agreeable place for free black people to live. Racism existed in the North too. A seriously ill African-American person could not obtain care in a hospital. It was not until 1841 that a few beds in Bellevue Hospital in New York City were set aside for "colored" patients. Accordingly, four times as many blacks as whites died during the yellow fever epidemic in Philadelphia, the City of Brotherly Love, in 1793. No one in power moved to train black physicians to serve their own people.

Far worse crimes against the Hippocratic oath occurred in the South, where some white male physicians used slaves as guinea pigs to try out new treatments and surgical methods. A piece of property, after all, had no right to protest. The infamous Nazi Dr. Mengele committed the same kinds of crimes against Jewish women in concentration camps during World War II.

Dr. J. Marion Sims is lauded in most medical history books as the father of gynecology. Only a few researchers mention that he tested his new surgical techniques on black slave women in Alabama in the 1840s. He purchased at least one of them, a slave named Anarcha. Dr. Sims performed *thirty* operations on Anarcha alone! Her suffering must have been unendurable. Anesthesia had been discovered in Europe, but was not yet used in the United States.

In 1853, his skills perfected, Sims moved to New York

City and opened a successful practice among well-off women patients. In 1855, he was appointed chief surgeon at the newly opened New York Woman's Hospital, founded by some wealthy society ladies. Sims performed his operations in the circus-like atmosphere of amphitheaters crowded with medical students and other spectators. This time his patients were poor immigrant Irish women, so-called charity cases. At prestigious Harvard, Sims was an object of near worship.[7]

There was one lone black woman who received her medical degree in 1864. One year before the end of the Civil War and fifteen years after Elizabeth Blackwell became the first woman doctor, Rebecca Lee graduated from New England Female Medical College. No other black women were admitted before the school closed in 1874.

Just prior to the Civil War, as antislavery sentiment increased, a few more African-American men practiced medicine. Their efforts and the atmosphere immediately after the Union victory left a tiny crack in the wall through which a handful of black women slipped.

Dr. Martin Delaney is probably the best-known trained black physician of that period. A free black, Delaney practiced among the poor black people of Pittsburgh and wrote and lectured against the prevalent theories of the racial inferiority of black people. As a student, Delaney had been one of the trio of African-Americans who requested permission to attend lectures at Harvard at the same time that Harriot Hunt was futilely applying.

Dr. James McCune Smith was another prominent black physician. He urged free blacks to join the abolitionist movement. Although the son of a better-off merchant, he still could not find an American medical school willing to take his tuition money. He attended the University of Glasgow and earned his medical degree in 1837, establishing a busy practice in New York and working long hours for the antislavery cause.

At war's end, thousands of ex-slaves wandered the war-torn South, most of them without shelter, food, or medical care. The long and terrible conflict had torn apart the whole economic life of the nation, and diseases raged, hitting the newly freed black people especially hard. To handle these problems, the federal government established the Freedmen's Bureau. Dr. Martin Delaney joined its staff. Setting up hospitals and schools was a priority. Two of the schools, Howard University Medical School, in Washington, D.C., and Meharry Medical College, in Nashville, Tennessee, are still in existence today.

Howard was chartered in 1868 and supported financially by the U.S. government. At first, white students outnumbered black students, and Dr. Alexander T. Augusta was the only black person on the faculty.

The men who ran Howard were aware that women's rights activists had worked hard for an end to slavery. Howard Medical School's Medical Alumni Association denounced discrimination against women "as being unmanly and unworthy of the profession," stating "we accord to all persons the same rights and immunities that we demand for ourselves."[8] In turn, the women pioneers, Elizabeth Blackwell, Harriot K. Hunt and Marie Zakrzewska encouraged African-American women to become doctors.

Howard's first two women graduates were white— Mary D. Speckman in 1872 and Mary A. Parsons in 1874. From 1870 to 1880, women accounted for 15 to 25 percent of Howard's Medical School enrollment. When Columbian's and National's medical departments opened to women, the number of Howard's white female students declined sharply. Black women, barred from most other colleges, continued to enroll at Howard.

Howard rapidly became disproportionately black and male, instead of the coeducational, racially integrated school its founders had anticipated. Part of the responsibility rested on the shoulders of a few administrators and faculty members. Silas Loomis, white dean of the

President Franklin Delano Roosevelt dedicates Howard University's chemistry building in 1936. Howard University was established by the Freedmen's Bureau in 1868 to help freed slaves. Aware that women's rights activists had worked for an end to slavery, Howard administrators admitted women from the university's beginning.

faculty and founder of the medical school, had been an abolitionist and strongly supported education for black men. His spirit of egalitarianism faltered, however, when it came to the question of higher education for women. He believed it would make them unable to bear and nurse normal children.

Two female students brought charges against the one black faculty member, Alexander Augusta, in 1873. They claimed that he had denied them materials in the anatomy laboratory he ran and had allowed some of the male students to insult them. Howard's administration quickly replaced Augusta.

Despite Howard's more enlightened attitude, when it came to the very few openings for three-month residencies at Freedmen's Hospital, they were all awarded to men. Teaching posts at the college were closed to women, but that was because the AMA prohibited such appointments.

Howard hired Isabel Barrows in 1871 as an ophthalmology instructor rather than as an assistant professor in order to circumvent this ruling. Nevertheless, AMA officials barred Howard's biracial delegation to its annual convention of 1872, citing Barrow's appointment and threatening to remove Howard University from its list of approved medical colleges. Howard did not appoint another woman for twenty years.[9]

Some leading black doctors decided to fight for the right to join medical societies, believing that membership would make it easier to break down the locked doors at other institutions. Choosing to target the leading society first, they put up a fight to integrate the AMA.

Even a resolution in the U.S. Senate in 1869 was unable to budge the AMA from its firm position of excluding women and black males. Inside the AMA, a civil-rights group formed to continue the struggle. White candidates who were known to support this minority were denied membership.

On January 15, 1871, in a Washington D.C. church, African-American physicians formed their own organization, the National Medical Society of the District of Columbia. Black male physicians had always been more accepting of women doctors than their white male counterparts had been. Victorianism and the Cult of Domesticity, after all, had not been present in the slave quarters of southern plantations. The roles played by black women in the struggle to survive slavery and then in the fight to abolish it earned them a large share of equality as well.

In its constitutional preamble, the National Medical Society stated its objective of "banding together for mutual co-operation and helpfulness, the men and women of African descent who are legally and honorably engaged in the practice of . . . Medicine, Surgery, Pharmacy and Dentistry."[10] Women participated in the NMA and some were elected as officers.[11] The society was an important model of cooperation and mutual support. Still, with so little power of their own, there wasn't much black male doctors could do to help the women physicians.

For almost a century, convention after convention of the AMA refused to enroll black or female members. Black physicians continued the struggle to open their own hospitals and schools, but even when they succeeded, their facilities were always smaller, their funds skimpier, and their staffs undertrained.

The situation was doomed to get worse before it got better. When Rutherford Hayes became the nineteenth president of the United States in 1876, he ordered the withdrawal of federal troops from the South. It was the beginning of the end of the meager Reconstruction programs, meaning more dashed hopes for black doctors.

On July 2, 1881, almost two decades after the Civil War, there appeared a solitary glimmer of hope for racial equality. The nation's twentieth president, James Abram Garfield, needed emergency medical attention, having just been shot by an assassin. Among the retinue of famous male physicians who surrounded the president's bed was one black doctor, the first ever to serve a president— Dr. Charles B. Purvis, surgeon-in-chief of the Freedmen's Hospital. Unfortunately, Garfield died after lingering with massive infections for eighty days. Germ theory was still not accepted, and as dozens of unscrubbed fingers probed deeply into the president's wound, they introduced thousands of bacteria into the wound.[12] No woman doctor was present, of course, black or white, but nevertheless Dr. Purvis's presence in the White House must have stirred hope that all the barriers, racial and sexual, would come down in the near future.

As the spirit of Reconstruction and reconciliation crumbled, such dreams were quickly scrapped. The Black Codes, known as "Jim Crow laws," segregating African Americans in every walk of life, were revived and strengthened in the South. The Freedmen's Bureau was abolished, and the all-black colleges had to limp along as best as they could without federal support. By 1890, the majority of the former Confederate states had repealed the civil-rights laws enacted during Reconstruction. Segregation was a legalized reality in the South.

With Freedmen's Bureau funds, Howard had developed a wide ranging choice of courses taught by well-known professors. It had erected new buildings and even subsidized lower tuition fees for poorer students. With the funding gone, the quality of education at Howard declined. In a desperate move to remain open, Howard offered fewer courses, shortened its term, and reduced tuition.

Meharry Medical College had been established solely for the education of black doctors. Since the majority of the black population still lived in the eleven states that had made up the Southern Confederacy, its location in Nashville made it easier for newly freed slaves to attend. Its first class of a dozen students was held in 1876 in an old wooden building once used as a barn. Eventually it was housed in a more appropriate four-story brick building financed by donations from four white brothers, the Meharrys.

Most of the students were poor and less educated than those attending Howard. From 1877 to 1890, Meharry graduated 192 black men. It was not until seventeen years after its opening, in 1893, the same year that Johns Hopkins admitted women, that two black women, Annie D. Gregg and Georgiana Esther Lee Patton, were handed their medical degrees.

By 1900, Howard and Meharry had graduated less than fifty African-American women, about 3 or 4 percent of their total graduates. The Woman's Medical College of Philadelphia, which had opened its doors to many women from abroad as well as minority women, had graduated about twelve black women by then, and perhaps another dozen were accepted at coed universities. All together they totaled a measly one hundred and fifteen by the turn of the century.[13]

Most of the members of this small legion of black women physicians were the daughters of privileged African-American parents. They had been well educated before beginning their medical studies, almost all of them in private schools. They could have established practices among families like their own, but several were deeply committed to improving the health conditions of their own people, choosing to live and practice in impoverished communities.[14]

Rebecca Lee, for example, said by some to be the first black woman doctor even though her degree was from Gregory's unchartered school (see chapter 3), left New England and returned home to Richmond, Virginia to work among newly freed blacks.[15] Rebecca J. Cole, the first black woman graduate of a chartered medical school, the Women's Medical College of Philadelphia, joined the Blackwells in 1869 at the New York Infirmary for Women and Children as a "sanitary visitor." Dr. Cole made house calls in slum neighborhoods, teaching women the basics of hygiene and disease prevention. The Blackwells' Tenement House Service was the earliest "visiting nurse" type program in the country. But Dr. Cole soon realized that the desperately poor southern blacks needed her services even more than the white immigrant women of New York. So she spent the remainder of the Reconstruction years in Columbia, South Carolina.

In later years, Cole and another woman physician founded the Women's Directory in Philadelphia, a medical and legal-aid center to help abandoned pregnant women. In her final years, Cole served as superintendent of Government House, a refuge for homeless children and old women in Washington, D.C.[16]

Black women became the first of *any* race to pass the state licensing examinations in four southern states[17]: Matilda Arabella Evans in South Carolina[18]; Halle Tanner Dillon Johnson, in Alabama[19]; Sara G. Boyd Jones in Virginia; and Verina Morton-Jones in Mississippi.[20] Three of them were graduates of the Women's Medical College of Philadelphia. These women were from middle-class and even wealthy families. Sarah G. Boyd Jones's father, George W. Boyd, was said to be the richest black man in Richmond, Virginia.

Rarely could an ex-slave woman overcome her economic and educational handicaps to study medicine, but Eliza Anna Grier managed to do it. Working her way slowly through Fisk University in Nashville, Tennessee, she then completed her studies at the Women's Medical College of Philadelphia, alternating work years with school years. She graduated in 1897, after seven years of struggle.[21]

It was even more difficult for black women than for white women to find internships. The Freedmen's Hospital in Washington, D.C., and the scattering of small all-black hospitals and clinics were not enough to handle the internship needs of African-American physicians of both sexes. They usually awarded their vacancies to hard-pressed black men. Women's hospitals usually turned away black female doctors in favor of whites.

Searching for alternatives to the impossible-to-get internships for meeting licensing qualifications, Dr. Matilda Evans turned her own home in Columbia, South Carolina into a small clinic and then established a full-scale hospital and nurses' training school.[22] Some black graduates fulfilled their internships by becoming resident physicians in segregated black colleges established during Reconstruction. For very low pay, they worked long hours taking care of the students and faculty and teaching health courses as well.

On September 6, 1901, twenty years after Dr. Purvis was invited to the White House, President William McKinley was the target of an assassin's bullet. The medical picture was almost the same. The chief surgeon in attendance was a high-society obstetrician who openly stated his conviction that the new germ theories were not to be taken too seriously. In eight days the president was dead, the victim of infection and blood poisoning. This time no African-American doctors or women doctors were present in the White House.[23]

The black doctors faced the harsh reality. Integration was not going to happen quickly. Perhaps it would never happen at all. They knew that they had to keep their own medical schools and societies alive, or before long there would be no black physicians in the nation. As white women doctors happily celebrated the Gilded Age of Medicine, entered coed medical schools, and closed the doors of most of the women's medical schools, half a dozen new medical colleges for blacks were opened.

It was undoubtedly a wise choice. In the opening decades of the twentieth century, new generations would be deeply influenced by the racism enveloping the nation. Black male doctors began to lose some of the small gains they had made at the same time that the hopes of white women doctors were being sharply diminished.

For black women interested in medical careers the situation became so grim that they had all but completely disappeared from the ranks of medicine by the time of the Flexner Report. In 1910, nearly 95 percent of employed black women were picking crops or working as maids, cooks, and nannies. Even low-paying factory jobs were difficult to get. With anti-black racism pervading all of society, factory owners preferred to hire white immigrants. A tiny group of black women, less than 2 percent, were professionals, most of them teachers who had graduated from black colleges and taught in segregated all-black schools.

The health situation of black people continued to deteriorate as their numbers increased to ten million by 1910. Poverty, malnutrition, and lack of education stalked their ranks, especially in rural areas, and there still were not enough black doctors or hospitals to begin to care for them. White and black doctors practiced mostly in cities. The NMA did its best to encourage young African Americans to study medicine, but reality discouraged them.

Most of the black institutions were on their last legs. Flexner's 1910 report tolled an even louder death knell for black medical colleges than it did for women's medical schools. In a chapter entitled "Medical Education of the Negro,"[24] Flexner advised black doctors to administer only to patients of their own race. He did not advise white physicians similarly. He severely criticized the black colleges, labeling them "ineffectual . . . sending out undisciplined men, whose lack of real training is covered up by the imposing M.D. degree." Only Meharry and Howard were worth saving, he concluded. Out of the seven black medical schools, the Flexner Report labeled five "in no position to make any contribution of value."[25]

Flexner did not offer aspiring black doctors the same comforting news that he had given to women—that medical schools were "open to women upon practically the same terms as men." Flexner knew full well that the black colleges were often the *only* opportunity for education available to black men. On black women, he had not a word to say.

Howard campaigned for funds and brought the university up to a high enough standard to earn the grade A accreditation. Meharry also plugged ahead, but the other black medical schools folded, creating an even greater shortage of black doctors.

Of 3,855 black doctors in the United States in 1920, less than half of one percent were women, most of them Howard or Meharry graduates. Internships remained almost impossible to find. Isabella Vandervall graduated at the head of her class at Women's Hospital in New York City in 1915. After seeing a bulletin board notice of an internship opening at the Syracuse Hospital for Women and Children, she applied. Her credentials were impressive and she was elated when a letter of acceptance arrived. She recounted her bitter experience later to an NAACP writer:

> *So to Syracuse I went with bag and baggage enough to last me for a year. I found the hospital; I found the superintendent. She asked me what I wanted. I told her I was Dr. Vandervall, the new interne. She simply stared and said not a word. Finally, when she came to her senses, she said to me: "You can't come here; we can't have you here! You are colored! You will have to go back."* [26]

By the late 1920s, there were only twelve accredited black hospitals and three white hospitals in the entire country accepting black interns and residents—all three white ones located in black ghettos in New York and Chicago. There weren't enough open slots to accommodate even the paltry one hundred black graduates each year.

Sometimes the rejections were straightforward. Dr. Lillian Atkins Moore received her answer from the medical director of a hospital when she applied for her internship after graduating from Women's Medical College of Philadelphia in 1893:

> *We are all your good friends and it is a most unpleasant thing to have to tell you that just because you are colored, we can't arrange to take you comfortably into the hospital. I am quite sure that most of the internes [sic] who come to us next year would not give us as good work as you are capable of doing . . .*[27]

The last on the totem pole of sexism and racism, the black woman physicians were shoved out of the backwaters of medicine and almost into oblivion.[28]

Little wonder that by the 1920s there were only sixty-five black women physicians in the entire United States, compared with 7,000 white women physicians. Twenty-five years after slavery ended, there had been almost double that number![29] Black male doctors remained stuck on the margins of medicine until the victories of the civil rights movement of the 1960s.

The severely depleted ranks of black women physicians continued to focus their energies on preventive medicine and health care for African Americans. Dr. Verina Morton-Jones became head worker at the Lincoln Settlement House in Brooklyn. Dr. Mary Etter Potter, a 1907 graduate of the National Medical College in Louisville, specialized in gynecology and obstetrics and served as the medical examiner for five black women's organizations in Louisville. Dr. Lilian Singleton Dove, a 1917 graduate of Meharry, was probably the first black female surgeon. Dr. Lucie Bragg Anthony, another Meharry graduate, class of 1907, became the supervisor of the segregated black county schools in Sumter, South

Carolina. She not only worked to improve the health of the youngsters in the area, but she gave her time to literacy classes and teacher training, helping to establish twenty-seven new schools. Dr. S. Maria Steward worked as a low-paid doctor among the poor and was an activist in the antilynching and suffrage movements as well.[30] None of these women seemed particularly concerned about accumulating wealth.

In Washington, D.C., when the Gilded Age of women doctors ended with a crash, white women physicians managed to carry out a few strategies to prevent the total collapse of their gains. When they were barred from clinical practice, they reached out to a handful of wealthy women and supportive males and established women's clinics. They could not compete with the universities and large urban hospitals that rejected their applications, but they were able to train the shrinking population of women medical students after the turn of the century.

Of the twenty-three black women who graduated from Howard between 1870 and 1900, only half actually practiced medicine. Not accepted by the white women's clinics, they had nowhere to turn. Not only were they everyone's last choice, but they found that most middle-class black professionals preferred white physicians. Many of them practiced medicine part-time and taught school during the day. Their medical degrees helped them achieve promotions and higher pay in the segregated Washington public school system. In 1913, of forty-eight black principals, thirty-three were women.[31]

White women physicians, unlike the early pioneers, were too busy preserving their own careers to notice the disappearance of black women from medicine. In Washington in 1909, eighteen white women formed the Women's Medical Society of Washington. They discussed medical issues and their own shrinking professional opportunities. Black women were not invited. By then, their numbers were so low they could not even

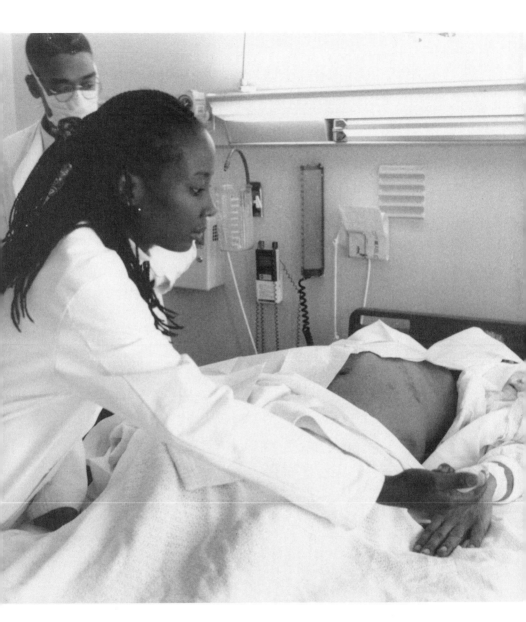

Dr. Rose-Marie Toussaint is a liver transplant surgeon on the staff of Howard University Hospital. The patient has undergone a transplant operation to receive a new liver.

form professional networks. The black medical societies also ignored them. By the 1930s only one black medical society out of four in Washington, D.C. listed a woman member.

All over Washington and other cities, professional organizations of every possible category sprang up. Black female office workers, teachers, and a few other professions, including doctors, organized self-help and mutual aid associations. These groups banded together to help one another financially, collecting and investing funds to provide for unemployment and death benefits. In 1900 more than three thousand black women participated in fifty such societies.

There were black elite clubs as well, composed of a tiny minority of wealthy black professionals. The Collegiate Alumnae Club founded in 1910 came under attack by other people in the black community for its snobbish membership requirements. The critics condemned the club for supposedly basing membership on a light complexion, sharp features, and elite family background.

The civil rights movement of the 1960s helped black professionals advance toward equal treatment. By then, black women physicians had to start again from almost ground zero.

In the 1970s, a new and more powerful women's-rights movement won enormous improvements in the lives of all women. It is impossible to say what the results would have been if women of all races and ethnic backgrounds had banded together earlier in the century to protect their hard-won gains. The history of women in medicine suggests that things could have been very different. For black women, the situation could not have been worse.

seven

NIGHTINGALE'S SLAVING ANGELS

They have only tried to be men, and they have succeeded only in being third-rate men.

—Florence Nightingale on the handful of pioneer woman physicians of her time.[1]

Just as doctoring is thought of as men's work, nursing is thought of as women's, despite the recent entry of some men into nursing. Medical care has long been divided into two distinct compartments. Doctors are the all-powerful healers, and nurses are the subordinate caretakers. The doctor arrives, diagnoses the patient, decides on a plan of treatment, gives his orders to the nurse, and leaves. The patient may not see him again for days. If there is an emergency, the nurse cannot make a move unless one or another doctor, even a brand-new intern, is summoned. Because of this master-servant relationship, nursing has long endured the problem of most so-called feminized professions—low status and low pay.

The first nurses date back to ancient societies where medicine men were in charge.[2] Female and male helpers played the role that modern nurses have played ever since. In the fourth century B.C., the Hindu physician Characka outlined the nurse's tasks: "Knowledge of the manner in which drugs should be prepared and compounded for administration, cleverness, devotion to the patient waited upon, and purity (both of mind and body)."[3]

King Asoka of Ceylon built many hospitals around 225 B.C. Those who cared for the sick were males called nurses. In other societies, slaves, both male and female, played the same role. Hippocrates, the famous Greek "father of medicine," mentioned assistants to physicians in his writings.

Among the early Christians, nuns were assigned to take care of patients in homes and hospitals. When the Crusades began in 1096, the elite men of the Knights Hospitalers, organized in Jerusalem about 1050, served as physicians. Their nurses were "Half-Knights," men from lower-status families.

After the twelfth century, hospitals were built in many cities. Often they were beautiful buildings, but inside, misery reigned. When wealthy and middle-class people fell ill, they preferred to trust their relatives and servants to see to their needs. The hospitals were meant for the poor, and they paid employees starvation wages. Accordingly, they were staffed with prostitutes who wanted to leave their harsh lives behind, elderly women who could find no other jobs, and alcoholics. They were supervised by men with no medical training. Patients often were left stretched out on vermin-infested mattresses on the filthy floors of airless rooms, hungry, neglected, and left to die alone or recover on their own.

From time to time there occurred efforts to improve the situation. In the fourteenth century, kings ordered the construction of thousands of hospitals. A huge contingent of wealthy women volunteered to visit the patients regularly. Over the centuries, all of these caretakers had one thing in common: They functioned as untrained servants, able to do little for most patients.

Later, permanent orders of nursing sisters were organized by Catholic and Protestant churches. The oldest nursing order in the world was that of the Augustinian Sisters, who served the *Hotel Dieu* in Paris, founded in 1605. Shut off from the outside world, they had no access to medical knowledge. Their job was largely that of cleaning women—scrubbing floors, washing clothes and bed linens, and bathing patients.

By the eighteenth and nineteenth centuries, the hospitals had barely improved since the Middle Ages. In England, with good reason, noblewomen took care of their families and servants at home. The rules of one hospital in 1789 give us an excellent indication of the conditions inside. Workers were banned from throwing "dirt, rags, or bones" from the windows, and warned that they would be "immediately discharged" if they "get drunk, neglect their patients, quarrel or fight with other nurses, or quarrel with men."[4] No wonder hospitals were still avoided by all who could find other care!

Reformers desperately tried to improve conditions. In 1825 the Quakers established a nursing order that placed student nurses in the hospitals of Edinburgh and London, and the churches sent in troops of barely trained nurse deaconesses.[5] Again, there was little change in the conditions of the suffering poor.

The woman who would change the face of nursing in Europe and the United States was then only a small child. Florence Nightingale was born in England in 1820.[6] Like many other women reformers, she came from a wealthy family. In keeping with the Victorian attitudes of the time, her father hired tutors to transform young Florence into an educated lady, hopefully to marry well and lead a life of ease.

The large estate where young Florence was raised was dotted with the humble cabins of her father's peasant work force. It was the custom then for charitable Christian ladies to pay visits to their tenant farmers when illness struck. They usually drove up in their carriages and waited while a servant left food at the door. As a teenager, Nightingale added her own innovation. Eyebrows were undoubtedly raised when young Florence actually entered the huts, fed the sick, and tidied their beds to make them comfortable.

Florence Nightingale was still single at twenty-four. An unmarried woman of that age was considered a permanent spinster, doomed to spend the rest of her life in the family home, embroidering, gossiping, and doing little else. Growing bored with her idle life, Nightingale confided her desire to work in a hospital to a visiting physician friend. He encouraged her, but her parents adamantly refused to grant their permission.

Five years later, on a trip abroad with a married couple, Nightingale arranged a visit to the Institute of Deaconesses of Kaiserworth, a hospital in Germany. When she returned home, Nightingale announced that she had arranged to study there for three months. To prevent gossip, her parents insisted that her trip remain a secret.

Finding the experience disappointing, Nightingale enrolled twice in English hospitals, but each time she was about to leave she was urged to stay at home to care for sick relatives. At last, in 1853, at the age of thirty-three, she was hired as superintendent of the Institution for the Care of Sick Gentlewomen in Distressed Circumstances, a hospital for aging governesses, companions, and other "ladylike" servants. Nightingale refused wages, considering it beneath her dignity to take money.

With great vigor, Nightingale proceeded to improve the hospital, making hot water available in every ward and placing a bell at each bedside so that patients could summon nurses. She also visited as many hospitals as she

Florence Nightingale, hospital reformer and English nurse, transformed the nursing profession and campaigned for proper treatment of soldiers wounded in war. The soldiers called her the Lady with the Lamp because she tirelessly made the rounds of the battlefront hospital wards at night with a lamp to comfort the wounded.

could in the area, accumulating data and developing a master plan for nurses' training.

In 1854, Turkey attempted to seize a Russian territory known as the Crimea. When the Russians appeared to be on the verge of victory, France and Great Britain feared for their empires and declared war on Russia. Thirty thousand British soldiers headed on ships through the Black Sea for an attack on the Russian naval base at Sebastopol. Because there was scarcely enough room for the men and their weapons, most of the medical equipment—anesthesia, painkillers, and even bandages—stayed behind. In the horrible battles that followed, care of the wounded was almost nonexistent.

The survivors were shipped back to Scutari, Turkey, where the hospital was already filled with thousands of cholera victims. Sewer gas leaked into the wards, and filth and blood were everywhere in the windowless rooms. Only a few doctors were on hand.

A journalist's articles about the scandalous treatment of the soldiers were published in England, and the public was outraged. They had learned that the Sisters of Charity were taking excellent care of French soldiers, and they demanded decent treatment for their own sons.

By then everyone had heard about the unusual gentlewoman, Florence Nightingale, who was stomping about England fuming over hospital conditions. The secretary of war urged her to organize a group of nurses and leave for Scutari. In October 1854, the government confirmed her as "Superintendent of the Female Nursing Establishment of the English General Hospitals in Turkey." She was the first English woman ever given a military assignment. A few days later, Florence Nightingale and thirty-eight nurses, about half from religious orders and fourteen from hospitals, embarked to face the horrors at Scutari. Later Nightingale expressed her dissatisfaction with her hospital recruits when she outlined requirements for nursing candidates: "Fat drunken old dames . . . must be barred."[7]

Even the filthy, cockroach-infested ship did not prepare Florence Nightingale for the horrors at Scutari. To make matters worse, she was treated coldly by local military officials who had been stung by the public criticisms. Nevertheless, she plunged into the work, laboring day and night, all the while listing the problems at Scutari as part of a plan for transforming all military hospitals. She demanded and received a battalion of soldiers from England to clean up the place (government officials knew that Nightingale would not hesitate to publicize a refusal). As death rates fell, Nightingale became the heroine of the British people. Ill herself, she was depressed by the idea that much work was left to be done all over the continent.

After two years, Nightingale returned home in a state of collapse. Queen Victoria invited her to Balmoral Castle in Scotland to thank her. Nightingale used the occasion to persuade the queen to use her influence for the establishment of a royal commission to improve the health of the British army in peace and war. A year later, when nothing had happened, Nightingale threatened to publish her descriptions of the conditions at Scutari and urge public pressure for her reform proposals.

Preferring secrecy, a government commission was quickly established to study Nightingale's report on army health conditions. Promises of improvements were made and then forgotten.

Childless herself, Nightingale wrote about her "children," the wounded soldiers she had nursed, and sharply criticized the wealthy men of England for turning their backs on them.

These people have fed their children on the fat of the land and dressed them in velvet and silk . . . I have had to see my children dressed in a dirty blanket and an old pair of regimental trowsers, and to see them fed on raw salt meat; and nine thousand of my children are dying, from causes which might have been prevented, in their foreign graves! But I can never forget![8]

Nightingale was frustrated and angry, and her poor health took a turn for the worse. She remained a semi-invalid for most of the rest of her life, campaigning for nurses' training and writing books on nursing.

During the height of Nightingale's popularity, a Florence Nightingale Fund was established to finance a training school for nurses. Directing the work from her bed, Nightingale organized the school. By 1869 the first group of fifteen nursing students enrolled at the Nightingale School for training nurses at St. Thomas's Hospital in London for a year-long course of formal study. The Nightingale graduates were soon heading up schools all over the world.

Justifiably, Nightingale is considered the founder of modern nursing. Her Victorian ideals, for better or worse, significantly shaped her theories and influenced nursing up to the present.

Most importantly, Nightingale willingly accepted the idea of complete subservience to male doctors as the key ingredient of nurses' training. Physicians feared that if nurses learned too much about the secrets of their art, they would function as competitors. When the doctors at Scutari seemed reluctant to allow the much-needed nurses to work, Nightingale assured them that she demanded absolute obedience from her staff, no matter what their opinion. Even under emergency conditions, Nightingale's nurses were not permitted to do anything without the direct order of a doctor.

This was not merely a concession to the doctors so that she and her nurses could go on with their work. Florence Nightingale had little use for those who fought for women's equality. In her writings she stated bluntly that she believed that women had caused their own problems. "I am brutally indifferent to the rights and wrongs of my own sex," she freely admitted.[9]

While Florence Nightingale was in the Crimea, Dr. "James" Barry, the woman who had disguised herself as a man in order to practice medicine, had come to evaluate the situation at Scutari. After Dr. Barry's death, when the news of her true identity spread throughout England, women's rights advocates were upset when Nightingale recalled the occasion of their meeting. Instead of complimenting Barry on her great deception or commenting on the forces that had caused such a drastic action, Nightingale had only nasty things to say about Barry:

> *(He) kept me standing in the midst of quite a crowd of soldiers . . . during the scolding I received, while (she) behaved like a brute. After (she) was dead, I was told (he) was a woman. I should say (she) was the most hardened creature I ever met.*[10]

Under the guidance of the Nightingale-modeled training programs, nurses everywhere remained caretakers in societies that grossly undervalued care. In the United States, the notoriously poor care of Civil War soldiers was the main impetus for doing something about nurses' training.

During the war, the famous American poet Walt Whitman searched for his missing brother, a soldier in the Union army. For three years Whitman journeyed through camp hospitals and makeshift clinics recording his experiences. In a mansion in Virginia in 1861, he described piles of amputated limbs and corpses. Stumbling through a maze of wounded young men, stretched out on makeshift pads on the floor, he comforted them and wrote letters for some. There were no nurses. A few soldiers who could move about and relatives who had found their injured loved ones cared for them.[11] Even so, when the famous reformer Dorothea Dix established the Sanitary Commission of the Union Army for nursing care on the battlefield, the Army Medical Corps protested.[12]

Dorothea Dix was born on her family's farm in Maine in 1802.[13] Marital difficulties plagued her parents' marriage, and Dorothea was shuttled between the home of her wealthy paternal grandmother in Boston and an aunt in Worcester, Massachusetts. After studying to become a teacher, she opened her own school in 1821.

When Dix's grandmother died, she left Dorothea a handsome inheritance. Like Florence Nightingale, Dix never married. Yearning to do something useful, in 1841 Dix volunteered to teach a Sunday school class at a woman's prison. Jail conditions shocked her. Mentally ill women were locked up with ordinary prisoners. Their jailers, who refused to light a fire for fear that the inmates would burn the place down, told Dix that lunatics could not feel the cold.

Dix had found her calling. By the end of 1842, she had visited every workhouse and prison in Massachusetts. She wrote a shocking report on her findings. Under her pressure, the state legislature passed the first laws in the nation on the care of the mentally ill.

Not satisfied to limit her work to Massachusetts, Dix traveled thousands of miles by stagecoach, steamboat, railroad and even horseback, trying to encourage legislation in almost every state. Then she urged the federal government to build institutions for the insane on public domain lands. Congress passed her proposed law, but President Franklin Pierce, a believer in states' rights, vetoed the bill. Dorothea Dix lost her first battle when Congress was unable to gather the votes to override the veto. Upset and discouraged, she took her reform work to Europe.

When the first guns of the Civil War were fired in April 1861, Dix returned and received a commission to recruit nurses for the Union army. Since there were no

*Dorothea Dix, American reformer who recruited
nurses during the Civil War and set up
hospitals at the battlefields.*

trained nurses and few hospitals, Dix did the best she could with scarce resources. She attempted to replace the old-style "nurses" with troops of disciplined, sober, older women, just as Nightingale had done. She proclaimed: "No woman under thirty need apply to serve in government hospitals. All nurses are required to be plain-looking women. Their dresses must be brown or black, with no bows, no curls, no jewelry and no hoopskirts."[14]

Few women applied, and those who did knew nothing about nursing, despite their "plain looks." As the war dragged on, it became obvious that untrained nurses could not even begin to deal with the enormous numbers of casualties.

When the Civil War ended, America's new middle classes, busy with their professional careers, urged the development of institutions they could trust with the care of their loved ones. A published description of Bellevue hospital in New York authenticated their drive for better hospitals. It read in part,

> When a visitor entered the ward . . . a little boy of five years old had just been operated upon . . . an old woman was sitting by him trying good naturedly to soothe his cries but doing nothing to staunch the blood which was flowing from the wound.[15]

As new hospitals opened to treat the expanding population and serve as learning centers for medical schools, wealthy women donated money and insisted that nursing schools be included in the new facilities. They also urged administrators to present nursing as highly respectable work in order to attract upper-class and middle-class women as nursing students. They were not very successful. No matter what recruiting propaganda said, nursing was viewed as low-paid heavy housework. Instead, the schools enrolled working-class women who preferred hospital work to grinding factory jobs.

The first formal nursing school was organized in 1871 at Dr. Marie Zakrzewska's New England Hospital for Women and Children. The "students" worked sixteen hours a day, seven days a week, washing, ironing, cleaning, and scrubbing. Of the forty enrollees at the New England Hospital in 1878, only three stuck out the year and earned their diplomas.

At most schools, the students received little instruction except an occasional lecture by a doctor in the evening or bedside instruction from a nursing superintendent during rounds. When too many women applied, they were sent to private homes to earn fees that the hospitals kept.

There can be little doubt that patient care improved as a direct result of the labor of thousands of nursing students. Cleanliness and attention no doubt helped the sick more than leeches and mercury preparations. But news quickly spread that the life of student nurses was terribly hard. In 1880, the United States Census listed 13,000 women as nurses. Only about 560 were graduates of hospital nursing courses.

When Johns Hopkins inaugurated a new "scientific" nursing school, leading nurses made efforts to professionalize their work, knowing that only then would it bring more respect and higher pay. An exhibit on nursing was presented at the Chicago World's Fair in 1893. Papers were presented criticizing the hospitals for sending their student nurses into private homes, making "philanthropists" of them and competing with graduate private-duty nurses who were looking for work.[16]

The criticisms apparently fell on deaf ears. As surgery became commonplace and hospitals became profitable, hundreds of in-hospital training schools were opened to meet the demand of patients paying for competent care. Barred from most occupations, many women applied.

By 1920 there were over 2,000 such schools graduating 17,500 nurses annually. But with hospitals continuing to use students as unpaid staff nurses, graduates often found jobs difficult to find.[17]

The same physicians who had placed barriers in the way of women physicians believed that nursing was a more natural occupation for women. They had objected that women would break under the strain of medical practice and would be endangered by contact with "vulgar and vicious" patients, yet they openly admired the public health nurses who entered "the slums of our city, . . . up the dark, dirty, rickety staircases of tenements."[18]

The *Woman's Journal* sarcastically criticized this double standard of male physicians. "Nurses are docile, submissive, and keep their proper place, while once let a woman study medicine and she thinks her opinion is as good as any man's."[19]

When an occasional nursing superintendent made an urgent decision because no doctor was available, she became the target of bitter complaints. Just as slaves were forbidden to learn reading and writing for fear that they would know too much and rebel, at first nurses were forbidden to read patients' medical histories. According to the first American nurse, Linda Richards, even at the New England Hospital for Women and Children, where the equal-rights advocate Dr. Zakrzewska presided, the medicine bottles had numbers instead of names so that the nurses had no idea of what they were dispensing.[20]

In 1908, when the AMA was reforming medical education, it recognized nurses as members of a learned profession. Later, this status would make it difficult for nurses to join unions in order to struggle for better conditions. Before World War I, most state legislatures had passed laws regulating nursing through licensing.[21]

In a Flexner-type report of 1923 called the Goldmark Report, Josephine Goldmark criticized the variations in quality of "trained" nurses and recommended a classification system in order to distinguish these new "professionals" from other nurses. She also strongly urged better working conditions and shorter work hours.[22]

It wasn't until the miserable days of the depression of the 1930s, when many nurses walked the sidewalks searching for work, that the American Nurses' Association and the National League of Nursing Education agreed to an eight-hour day to share the available work and ease unemployment. They also accepted the nursing education standards set out in the Goldmark Report.

The depression also brought a victory for one trained nurse, Margaret Sanger, who had been the center of an enormous controversy since 1912. Most histories of nursing fail to even mention her, but there were very few people in the nation who did not have strong opinions on Sanger's campaign for birth control.

Her life work started when a patient of hers died as a result of an illegal abortion. Until 1873, when Congress passed laws banning birth control, abortion had been perfectly legal, although inaccessible to most women.

Sanger went on speaking tours around the nation, much as Dorothea Dix had done. When she opened the first birth control clinic in Brooklyn, New York, in 1916, the police burst into the premises and arrested her. It was the first of eight arrests, and years of struggle lay ahead. Finally, in 1936, when poverty swept over the nation and more physicians advocated birth control, the laws against contraceptives were struck down. Margaret Sanger was a heroine to all women who wanted to make their own childbearing decisions. Throughout the country, women's clinics were named in her honor.[23]

By the late 1930s, a hierarchy of nurses worked in the hospitals. At the top of the pyramid were the registered nurses with the most training. Licensed practical nurses with less schooling assisted them. Lowest on the totem pole were the often untrained nurses' aides, many of them immigrants or black women.

Margaret Sanger, a nurse activist who campaigned for women's rights to birth control and abortion. Sanger began her work in 1912 after one of her patients died from an illegal abortion. Today many women's health clinics are named for her.

Black women trying to enter nursing schools confronted almost as much resistance as those who had aspirations to become doctors. In the South, nursing schools were closed to them. In the North, only a sprinkling of schools admitted them. Even at the New England Hospital for Women and Children, it was only because of Dr. Zakrzewska's insistence that the nursing school charter called for the admission of *one* Jewish and *one* black woman each term.[24]

The first black trained nurse in the United States, Mary Eliza Mahoney, received her diploma there in 1879. She was one of a handful of black women admitted over the years. In 1899, when a more generous quota was allowed, a half-dozen black nurses followed in her footsteps.

During the Gilded Age, when woman doctors were entering coeducational medical schools and closing down their own medical colleges, openings grew scarce. Black nursing students began flocking to newly developing all-black training centers.

Just as the male medical societies had barred woman doctors, the white Nurses' Associated Alumnae, later renamed the American Nurses' Association, made it all but impossible for black graduate nurses to attain membership. In 1908, a few dozen black nurses formed the National Association of Colored Graduate Nurses. Over the years its leaders worked hard to help black women become nurses.

For the first half of the twentieth century, not only African Americans in the medical professions but all black people could justifiably feel that nothing was moving for them. When the United States joined the Allies to fight the First World War, which was supposed to "end all wars," there was no question that black men would be conscripted into the army. Many resented serving in segregated units, but others thought it would give them an opening to prove that blacks were also brave and competent Americans.

Three hundred and fifty-six African-American doctors were commissioned as medical officers for the black troops, and they organized base hospitals for them. Black nurses were excluded by the Army, but during a serious influenza epidemic in 1918, desperate for nurses, the Army finally admitted eighteen black women into its nursing corps and sent them to segregated quarters in two northern Army camps. When the epidemic ended, they were discharged.

When injured black soldiers were brought home, where to treat them became a growing problem. Veterans hospitals were filled with wounded white soldiers, and only a few facilities opened some segregated wards for the black veterans. After an NAACP campaign, the Veterans Bureau and Tuskeegee Institute joined together in 1921 to build a hospital on land owned by Tuskeegee. Plans were announced and carried out to open the new facility "with a full staff of white doctors and white nurses with colored nursemaids for each white nurse, in order to save them from contact with colored patients!"[25]

After two years of protest by black organizations, a harassed and pressured President Harding in 1923 ordered special civil service examinations for jobs at the Tuskeegee Veterans Hospital. Perhaps some believed that black nurses and doctors would fail the tests, but they were mistaken. The superintendent resigned in protest as more black medical personnel joined the staff, and the Ku Klux Klan burned crosses and paraded in front of the facility, objecting to any racial mixing. A short while later, the decision was reached to use an all-black staff.

Most other hospitals that treated black patients also refused to hire black doctors and nurses. Harlem Hospital in New York City was one such place. It had been overcrowded almost from its opening day in 1907. When black southerners poured into Harlem from the South in search of factory work during World War I, the hospital was strained far beyond capacity. Responding to demands that black doctors and nurses join their staff, the administrators appointed one token African-American male doctor as clinical assistant in the outpatient department. Four white physicians resigned.

Public outrage and organized protest brought changes in the mid-1920s. When a private investigation revealed that black patients were poorly treated at Harlem Hospital, it became a hot political issue since by then a sizeable number of black people voted. Because of pressure from black voters and their white political allies, public hearings were held that led to the opening of a training school for black nurses and the hiring of black nurses and doctors at Harlem Hospital.

The Great Depression of the 1930s was a leveler and unifier. White and black men and women alike stood on bread and soup lines without jobs or hope, trying only to survive. Furniture was piled up on sidewalks all over the nation, in white and black neighborhoods, as working people could not pay their rent and families were thrown out on the streets.

In the midst of their mutual suffering, a new understanding swept over some of them. Unemployment councils and movements demanding relief were integrated. White and black workers joined together to form unions. They demanded government projects to alleviate the suffering. New Deal agencies under Franklin Delano Roosevelt's presidency were organized without regard to race. Poverty was the only requirement.

Some black nurses benefited from these developments. The Rosenwald Fund, a Jewish foundation that contributed to the National Association of Colored Graduate Nurses and fought for the passage of health legislation, was an important ally. New public health organizations employed about a hundred black nurses to serve in the African-American ghettos.

As late as 1941, there were only fourteen so-called integrated nursing schools, where a handful of black women students lived in segregated rooms in isolated areas of the hospitals. Most African-American women enrolled in twenty-nine all-black schools.

When World War II began, the National Medical Association met with Army officials and presented them with data on available black medical personnel. It wasn't until two years after Pearl Harbor that five hundred black physicians were allowed to enter the armed forces. The National Association of Colored Graduate Nurses battled for a similar right. "No Negro Nurses Wanted" was the heading of an editorial in a black publication.[26]

Because of severe shortages of nurses, however, about 500 black nurses were permitted to serve by the end of the war. Although the super-racist theories of Nazi Germany shocked most Americans, black troops and medical personnel continued to be segregated.

Dr. Charles Drew, a black doctor who was the leading expert on the subject of blood collection, preservation, and transfusion, was made assistant director of blood collection for the Army and Navy. But even this honor was tarnished with insult. The blood collected for the wounded servicemen was segregated into white blood and black blood, and Charles Drew, who knew better than any other scientist that this was ridiculous, had to make sure that the rule was not broken.

Nevertheless, the fact that a million black men served during World War II had an enormous impact on the future. As part of the liberating army that came to free Europe from the yoke of tyrants, black soldiers were equally welcomed as heroes. When they returned home, their expectations of fair treatment had risen. At the same time, many of the people of Africa and Asia were demanding freedom from their colonial masters. Black leaders became less and less interested in having "separate but equal" facilities that usually were separate but unequal.

Under public pressure, the Veterans Administration

Dr. Charles Drew, African-American physician who in 1940 discovered the method for preserving blood plasma used for transfusions to the sick and injured. His discovery saved the lives of countless soldiers on the World War II battlefields. Ironically, the segregated army also segregated blood supplies, although Dr. Drew, a black scientist, knew there was no legitimate rationale for this practice.

gradually integrated its hospitals. In 1946, the U.S. Senate passed the Hill-Burton Act to build hospitals, which included a clause authorizing the use of federal funds for the construction of segregated hospitals. A newly created organization, the Medical Committee for Human Rights, lobbied and won the repeal of the morally repugnant clause. Hospitals built with federal aid were legally required to open their doors to black patients, physicians and nurses.

When most chapters of the American Nurses' Association permitted black nurses to join their organization, the National Association of Colored Graduate Nurses voted to dissolve in 1951, after 43 years. Black doctors benefited from this move. The AMA, American Hospital Association, and other stalwarts of the medical profession could no longer resist the tide of history and reluctantly admitted black physicians.

Black women were entering nursing in increasing numbers, their ranks growing from about twenty-five hundred in 1910 to nine thousand in 1954. By the early 1960s, although the situation had improved, black physicians and nurses were still at a serious disadvantage. They were paid less and had fewer opportunities for advancement. Just as white women doctors had debated the continuation of separate medical schools for women, after 1954, when school integration became the law of the land, black nurses debated whether nurses' training schools for black women should continue. Several shut down, but a few new ones opened up.[27]

Most nurses, white or black, did not yet discuss the question of job status and responsibility. That would have to wait for a new women's-rights movement (see chapter 9). Florence Nightingale's humiliating rules continued to govern nursing with an iron hand.

eight

THE ALLIED HEALTH PROFESSIONALS— WOMEN IN A MAN'S WORLD

What unites women is their common femaleness, their distrust of organized medicine, their belief that self-knowledge of anatomy and bodily functions can be liberating, their insistence that women control the means of reproduction—and thus their lives.[1]

—Sheryl Burt Ruzek

After World War II, rapid technical advances created an array of new health professions and an expansion of the old ones. Once again, in the United States at least, scientific "professionalization" meant more men at the top and women at the bottom.

The male "family" dentist sent his patients off to male orthodontists, periodontists, or dental surgeons for braces, gum surgery, and tooth-extraction. In his office, dental hygienists—usually female—cleaned people's teeth and handled X rays.

Family drugstores almost disappeared and were replaced by huge national chains and even supermarkets, where pharmacists were tucked away behind a prescription counter. Ophthalmologists, optometrists, and other eye specialists no longer checked out people's vision in the rear of an eyewear store, but had offices equipped with female assistants and impressive-looking machinery.

In the hospitals, an army of female health workers dominated the scene. A wide array of new health specialties was rapidly becoming indispensable for patient care. No longer did a doctor work at a bedside, accompanied by interns and a few nurses. By the 1960s, doctors examined patients and ordered them shipped off to various wings of the buildings. There beehives of nursing aides, physicians' assistants, medical assistants, orderlies, medical records clerks, laboratory technicians and medical technologists performed X rays, sonograms, CAT scans, cardiopulmonary function tests, myriad blood tests, and other advanced and expensive procedures on the patients.

In the hospital kitchens, dietitians and nutritionists instructed teams of cooks. In gym-like surroundings, physical therapists helped patients recover the use of injured muscles, joints, and limbs. Amputees and brace wearers no longer had fittings in a shop run by a craftsman and his apprentice. They were measured by men newly licensed in prosthetics and orthotics. Often a hospital pharmacy filled prescriptions for discharged patients to take home. Psychotherapists, psychiatrists, and other mental health workers were on hand to assist patients and their families to adjust to illness and death.

In these far more complex settings, doctors remained the kings of a far larger kingdom. Until the early 1970s, women physicians remained at the lowly 4 to 5 percent of the profession that they had dropped to after the Gilded Age. Although most physicians knew little about the workings of these new high-tech skills, they remained decisively in charge of everything and everyone. Most of the "everyones" were female, and all of them had been taught total obedience to the "King Doctors."[2]

The pecking order was pretty much the same in all of the newer health categories. Occupational therapy as a distinct profession, for example, started after World War I to service disabled veterans. After World War II, when many more broken young men returned home, rehabilitation services for the handicapped were demanded, and several related professions such as physical therapy and prosthetics and orthotics developed. They were highly specialized fields, and it was impossible for most doctors to develop real knowledge of their methods. Yet, as early as 1922, graduating occupational therapists pledged to "walk in upright faithfulness and obedience to those under whose guidance I am to work."[3] This rule still applies today. Physical therapists are permitted to treat only patients referred by physicians. Most other health professionals function under the same restrictions.[4] This system costs patients millions of dollars annually in additional fees.

Like nurses, other health care professionals are caught in a very peculiar contradiction. Despite the fact that King Doctor is in charge, they can be sued for malpractice. On the one hand, they are not supposed to question the authority of the doctor's orders. On the other hand, they may be blamed if something goes wrong.

By the early 1970s, three-quarters of the nation's three million health workers were women, while almost all administrators, directors, and physicians were men. The so-called allied health workers were generally low paid. Minority women, mostly black or Hispanic, having no money for further training and little encouragement, comprised more than half of the lowest-paid hospital service and clerical workers.

Women served as aides, orderlies, cooks, practical nurses, office clerks, and as cleaning women on the housekeeping staff. The number of practical nurses almost doubled between 1960 and 1970. The incomes of those with several children often fell below the government's already low poverty cut-off line, making them eligible for supplementary welfare even though they worked full time.

Middle-class white women usually became Registered Nurses, dietitians, physical therapists, medical technicians and medical social workers. There was little communication or solidarity between members of the various groups. Nurses were taught to keep the other health workers in line, and make sure that the workers understood that doctors were the ultimate authorities.

As the underpaid feminized work force grew by leaps and bounds, the power of about half a million physicians, administrators, health corporation managers, medical school faculties and insurance company executives increased. This created what became known as labor problems.

In the 1960s unions began organizing in hospitals. One of the first was Local 1199, the Health and Hospital Workers Union, in New York City. Because nurses were difficult to organize, members were recruited among the lowest-paid workers, those who did not consider themselves professionals. In 1964 the union formed a separate guild for clerical, technical and other "skilled" professionals.

Higher-paying professions, such as dentistry and pharmacy, that usually operate outside of hospital settings, excluded women for many years. Pharmacy, now a feminized profession, has a very different history from nursing.[5]

In Colonial times and right after the American Revolution, people who compounded and dispensed medicines were called apothecaries. They and their apprentices sold their preparations to domestic healers and physicians or tended patients themselves in their shops. A few women were drug-shop owners.

When doctors' prescriptions became commonplace after 1800, pharmacies became a retail enterprise linked to medicine. By then, retail stores were run almost exclu-

District 1199 Hospital Workers Union organizes nurses, technicians, cleaning staff — most of the employees of the hospital, with the exception of doctors and management. The union membership is about 90 percent female.

sively by men. Pharmacists bought crude plant material and chemicals in huge drums and manufactured their own medicines. Apprentices labored long hours grinding, mixing, and packaging herbal and chemical concoctions. They often slept in the store, ready to answer the bell if someone needed medicine late at night. White women, of course, were considered far too "delicate" for such work.

Before the Civil War, pharmacists were looked upon as tradesmen rather than professionals. In order to earn a diploma from a school of pharmacy, they merely had to pay a fee and prove they had fulfilled a four-year apprenticeship. After the Civil War, drug manufacture shifted rapidly to factories. As the new era of professionalism took hold, pharmacy schools spread. They often competed for enrollments and welcomed female applicants.

Entering the schools was one thing, but finding good jobs after graduating was another. Only thirty-four women were listed in the 1870 Census among over seventeen thousand "traders and dealers in drugs and medicines." Even during the Gilded Age, less than a handful of women pharmacy school graduates worked in the field.

Since most jobs were available in community drugstores owned by men, women became the victims once more of gender stereotyping. Most male pharmacists simply did not believe that women had the emotional stability to deal with customers. The few who found employment worked in hospitals and laboratories, away from the public, or in village drugstores in rural areas, where men and women were accustomed to working together.

Joseph P. Barnum hired women apprentices to work in his pharmacy in Louisville, Kentucky. Some of them were widows of Confederate army soldiers. Barnum encouraged them to attend the Louisville College of Pharmacy. When their applications were refused, he set up the Louisville School of Pharmacy for Women in 1884, closing it shortly after Louisville College admitted women six years later.

Pharmacists' organizations were less restrictive than medical societies. At its 1879 meeting, the American Conference of Pharmaceutical Faculties decided to admit women into membership. Nevertheless, with little improvement in the employment situation, women refrained from considering pharmacy a profession. Laws restricting work hours for women were a further excuse for the emerging drugstore chains to reject their applications. In 1950, only four out of one hundred pharmacists were female. Two decades later, the situation had changed dramatically, as we shall see in the next chapter.

Although many women were encouraged to train as dental assistants and hygienists, and there were more than enough jobs to go around, women were a rarity in dentistry far longer than in other medical professions. Until 1979, less than 2 percent of dentists were women. In stark contrast, in several European countries after World War II, women comprised one-fourth to more than half of the dentists.[6] They are considered ideal for that profession, where deft fingers and nurturing behavior, both so often ascribed to "delicate" women, are important.

Similarly, there were few women veterinarians. Although many women were especially fond of animals and most pets are small in size, women were told that they lacked the "strength" to deal with "large" or "dangerous" animals.[7] Yet many girls in rural areas grew up handling horses and livestock.

Beginning in the late 1950s and mushrooming in the 1960s, social-protest movements against inequality and war swept the country. Black people, the most oppressed group, paved the way with the civil-rights movement led by men like Dr. Martin Luther King, Jr., and women like Fannie Lou Hamer. White sympathizers joined blacks at segregated lunch counter sit-ins and voting-rights campaigns. Courageous students of all ages participated. Despite murders, clubbings, and FBI harassment, they succeeded in ending legalized segregation in the South.

As war escalated in Vietnam, an antiwar movement was also born. Internationally, people of all races and ethnic groups and from all walks of life joined in mammoth demonstrations to protest United States intervention in Southeast Asia. When the majority of Americans turned against the Vietnam War, President Lyndon Baines Johnson withdrew from the presidential race in 1968, and politicians began jumping on the antiwar bandwagon.

As the political power of mass actions independent of the political parties became more apparent, other minority groups organized too. Native Americans founded the American Indian Movement (AIM); Puerto Ricans, the Young Lords; Chicanos (Mexican Americans) the La Raza Unida.

Women worked within all the new mass organizations, but they were seldom placed in leadership positions. Just as many men had mocked the women of the earlier feminist movements, "brothers" in the 1960s social movements often belittled women's concerns.

Many movement women wanted fairer treatment and faster action on a variety of issues. Between 1968 and 1970, mostly white and middle-class women began organizing women's liberation groups all over the nation. In so-called consciousness-raising groups, they concentrated on educating women to reject sex role stereotypes. During these meetings, women discussed such matters as their ignorance of their own bodies and their lack of trust in the male medical establishment. In many ways they were duplicating the classrooms of the Women's Physiological societies of the 1840s.

These groups inspired the birth of self-help groups and feminist health clinics.[8] They talked about their experiences with doctors, how their questions were ignored, how they were treated like children, how they were subjected to often unnecessary medical procedures like cesarean sections and expensive hormone treatments. They confessed that they were tired of being described as neurotic and being told that their complaints were psychosomatic—"all in your mind"—while men were taken more seriously when they were ill.

Finally, they discussed a more delicate subject: their lack of control over unwanted pregnancies. They took turns telling long-suppressed horror stories about their experiences with illegal abortions. Soon they were organizing huge rallies and marches to demand the right to safe and legal abortions.

Beginning in 1971, women across the country learned how to perform their own gynecological exams using an educational book self-published by the Boston Women's Health Collective, called *Our Bodies, Ourselves.* Two years later a major publisher reissued the book. A million copies of the first edition were sold and the book has been revised several times over the years.[9]

Publicity about the new feminist movement brought problems. Leading members of the self-help groups were placed under police surveillance, and some were arrested and tried for practicing medicine without a license.[10] World-renowned anthropologist Margaret Mead wryly commented in a newspaper interview that it was called "progress" when "men began taking over obstetrics and they invented a tool that allowed them to look inside of women" but that "when women tried to look inside themselves, this was called practicing medicine without a license."[11]

As women in the movement gained self-confidence, they rejected the idea that they were naturally passive and functioned best under male leadership. The first all-women's anti-Vietnam War demonstration took place in January 1968 in Washington, D.C. On August 26, 1970, a coalition of the National Organization of Women (NOW) and women's liberation groups celebrated the fiftieth anniversary of woman suffrage with rallies and marches across the nation. In New York City, for the first time in half a century, twenty thousand women paraded down Fifth Avenue. They were demanding equal opportunity in education and employment, child-care centers, and legalized abortion. Many women health care workers, physicians included, marched proudly that day. It is possible that a few of them knew that the earliest feminists had paved the way in the 1840s for the pioneer women doctors.

But it is doubtful that any of them so much as guessed how their new "second wave" of feminism—actually the third after the 1840s feminists and the suffragists—would change the lives of all Americans.

Things would never be the same for anyone, not even "King Doctor."

nine

RING IN A VICTORY—
RING OUT A WARNING

I don't think that the status of women in the profession is changing noticeably. You don't see the
women as the deans of medical schools or as
chairmen of departments of internal medicine.
They're still in the lower ranks of the profession. . . .

> —Dr. Vanessa Gamble, in 1978, at
> the height of the euphoria over
> women's inclusion in the world of
> medicine.[1]

As state after state lifted their bans on abortion, the
women's-liberation movement grew bolder and stronger
and started pushing for equality for women in all walks of
life. The largest group, NOW, next turned its energies
toward the task of state ratification of an Equal Rights
amendment (ERA) to the U.S. Constitution.

Serious differences emerged within the group. Some
rank-and-file members argued with the leadership that if
NOW wanted to attract white and non-white working-
class women to its cause, then it should concentrate on
issues that mattered most to these women—a national
health care system, child-care centers, housing, and
job training.[2] Even if two-thirds of the states ratified
the ERA, which appeared to be unlikely, court suits

would be necessary to enforce the amendment. Anti-discrimination suits could already be pressed under the 1965 Civil Rights Act, the equal protection provisions of the Constitution, and the Equal Pay Act.

The leadership position won. However, despite many years of expense and effort, NOW was not able to win ratification of the ERA in a sufficient number of states, and the amendment was defeated. Exhausted from the massive ERA effort, the women's movement did not mount other national campaigns. Meanwhile, economic hard times brought increased misery for millions of already hard-pressed families.

The facts indicate that the women's-liberation movement brought about enormous changes in the lives of middle-class and professional women. In 1970, the year of the largest women's demonstrations, Congress held its first hearings on inequality in medical school admissions. The Women's Equity Action League (WEAL) filed a class-action suit on behalf of all women against every medical college in the nation. That case and many other court suits led to federal laws outlawing gender discrimination as a violation of the equal protection provisions of the Constitution.

Medical schools quickly instituted "affirmative action" programs. Originally designed to encourage "disadvantaged persons," mainly minority students, to enter the health professions, affirmative action now included women in the disadvantaged categories. Years of not-so-secret quotas finally disappeared. By the late 1970s and early 1980s, one-third of medical school graduates were women.[3]

Possibly in an effort to minimize the obvious effectiveness of independent mass-action movements, some have claimed that a severe shortage of physicians in the late 1960s was the main factor in the decision to admit more women to medical schools. When several major teaching hospitals in Boston, for example, accepted female surgical interns for the very first time, they denied that their decision had been caused by outside pressure from women's-rights advocates. They characterized the timing of their sudden decision as an "accident, a pure accident."[4]

The facts tell a very different story. Despite the need for more doctors in the 1960s, *before* women marched, medical schools were in no hurry to voluntarily admit more of them. In 1967, for example, the Division of Medical Education of the AMA proposed that existing medical schools should be expanded and new schools should be built, but there was no mention of increasing the number of women students.[5] Female enrollment figures remained fixed at the same 7 to 9 percent recorded in 1961.[6]

Dr. Vanessa Gamble, an African-American woman, graduated from high school in 1968 and wanted to study medicine. In later years, Dr. Gamble realized that the power of the civil-rights movement and the women's-liberation movement helped turn her dream into a possibility. She commented to interviewers compiling oral histories of women physicians that the authorities were forced to start treating minorities more fairly:

> *Now they say they are dedicated to having more minorities in medicine. I don't know that if it weren't for things that happened in the sixties— in many cases they were forced to—that they would have started doing it.[7]*

Male applicants to medical schools had outnumbered females eight to one until the mid–1970s. By 1985, the ratio was only two to one. Although graduating women still had fewer choices of internships than men, the doors of most hospitals had opened to them. The success of these new women of medicine gave others the courage to forge ahead. Medical studies were no longer an exercise in futility.[8]

Other health professions opened their doors to

women. The New York State College of Veterinary Medicine at Cornell University, for example, without crediting the woman's movement at all, stated that with the use of "sleepy guns" (projectiles filled with tranquilizers), women would be able to handle dangerous animals. By 1981, half the graduate veterinarians were female.

Women seemed more reluctant to enter the traditionally male fields of dentistry, optometry, and podiatry. People in these professions are almost always self-employed and must spend a great deal of money to open and equip an office. Women usually have less access to loans and other assistance. A recent study concluded that women usually prefer to work in group situations of equality and cooperation rather than working alone and employing others.[9] Perhaps early training in taking orders from authoritarian male figures shaped this dislike of being a boss. Even so, the ranks of women students in these fields grew from less than 5 percent in 1976 to more than 25 percent by 1988.[10]

In pharmacy, women made the most rapid gains. With chain drugstores no longer able to get away with discriminatory hiring practices, women enrolled rapidly in colleges of pharmacy, making up almost 57 percent of all graduates by the end of 1987.[11]

Nursing remained an almost completely female profession, but it was not left untouched by the women's movement. "Nursing is going though its own process of 'consciousness raising,' " wrote a nursing school dean in 1973.[12] Regular articles with titles like "Sex Discrimination: Nursing's Most Pervasive Problem" and "Nurses' Rights" appeared in the American Nurses' Association's journal. Nurses began to realize that as the largest single group of health professionals, they had the power to improve the health care system and change their own work conditions.

Nurses started struggling to break with the Nightingale model of subservience. At the 1973 convention of NOW, a group of nurses met together for the first time to talk about their special problems. The following year, the American Nurses' Association established the Nurses' Coalition for Action in Politics, with the stated goal of promoting improved health care.

Unions also made important inroads among nurses. In June 1974, four thousand nurses went on strike at San Francisco area hospitals. Their main demand was the right to help determine patient care.[13]

Legislatures in several states passed laws expanding nurses' responsibilities. In New York State, the powerful Medical Society and Hospital Association attempted to block the passage of legislation allowing nurses to provide ". . . care supportive to or restorative of life and well being," despite the fact that the law made it clear that nurses could only carry out "medical regimens prescribed by a licensed . . . physician or dentist."[14] After several thousand nurses marched and chanted in front of the state capital in Albany, the bill was passed in a flash.

In rural areas, where shortages of doctors were severe, some states authorized nurse practitioners to work with considerable independence. They are now permitted to administer medications under a long-term physician order, and they also emphasize preventive measures like health education and regular physical examinations. Many nurse-practitioners believe that they have gone far toward resolving the separation between the curing and caring roles.[15] They resemble most closely the women healers of the ancient world and Colonial America.

The once respected and almost vanished art of midwifery has enjoyed a renaissance in the wake of the women's movement.[16] As the birth process came under the thumb of medical technology, pregnant women were hooked up to monitors and intravenous bottles filled with painkilling and labor-inducing drugs. Childbirth was being treated like a disease, increasing numbers of women protested. They wanted a return to the days of drug-free births with a knowledgeable, comforting person present during labor.

A growing number of middle-class and poorer women turned to midwives when well-publicized data proved that in countries where more births are handled by midwives, maternal and infant injuries and deaths are much lower. Furthermore, doctor-attended birthing had become prohibitively expensive. Midwives charge far less than obstetricians and in-home births eliminate the high costs of hospital stays.[17]

In the 1990s, it seemed at a glance that women in medicine were on their way to full equality. The decline and fall of the Gilded Age a century earlier was ancient history, known only to a handful of scholars. Even many who were aware of the opening-and-closing-doors phenomenon believed women could never again be pushed down. But a closer look at the rosy picture revealed several danger signs.

In her best-selling book *Backlash*, Susan Faludi presented evidence that women's gains declined during the recession of the 1980s. In the seventies, women struggling for equal pay wore buttons proclaiming that they earned only 59 cents to a man's dollar. These figures slowly improved, but by 1988, female college graduates could legitimately wear the old 59-cent button again. The wages of African-American, Hispanic, and older women of every race had improved less to begin with, and in recent years the gains they had made disappeared completely.[18]

Faludi also claimed that women's gains in medicine and other elite professions had been exaggerated. Furthermore, she said, they were achieved by the early 1980s "and barely budged since."[19]

New women physicians quickly realized that these institutions remained firmly under the control of male physicians and administrators with the power to hire, fire, promote, and decide on salaries and work rules. Even token women administrators could do very little for them. Consequently, women physicians today are only half as likely as males to establish successful practices of their own. Twice as many work as employees of clinics, hospitals, and other health facilities.[20]

When Dr. Mary Howell was appointed associate dean at Harvard Medical School in 1972, she optimistically believed that she could play an important role in the lives of women physicians and medical students. In 1975, she left her prestigious post. In "An Open Letter to the Woman's Health Movement," she explained the reasons for her disillusionment:

> *The problems that we are struggling against, of disadvantage and deprivation of privilege, are not the problems of individuals . . . [we] are not helped, and may be hurt by token appointments. Only when our representatives have a real voice in decisions will changes come about.*[21]

A few years after Dr. Howell's resignation, it appeared that the number of women administrators had increased impressively. The reality was that most of them worked in lower-paying, small, often rural facilities or not-for-profit institutions. Furthermore, these women administrators most often supervised female work forces in departments such as housekeeping, dietetics, and nursing. Only a small fraction were found in prestigious policy-making positions.[22]

The latest government data reveal an even further decline. Women held only 12.7 percent of administrative jobs of *any* kind in 1986.[23] Women comprised only 18 percent of practicing physicians in 1993.[24]

In all health-field categories, problems persisted and new danger signs emerged. Despite nurses' increased activism in the 1970s, confusion remained over their status. As the health care of Americans declined, the number of malpractice suits increased. The representatives of insurance companies, almost always men, had the power to end careers.

With an increase in the numbers of specialty nurses

Dr. Celia Maxwell is an expert in infectious diseases and tropical medicine at Howard University Hospital. She is consulting with a colleague in the Surgical Intensive Care Unit. Dr. Maxwell is an exception in health care, where black and Hispanic women are predominant in the lowest-paid service sectors of the system.

like nurse-practitioners and nurse-midwives, as well as the appearance of new health professionals such as Physicians' Assistants (PAs), there exists even more confusion over the educational requirements, responsibilities, and status of nurses. In most states, PAs, the majority of them male, are licensed after one year of training and one year of apprenticeship to a doctor. Although most Registered Nurses are graduates of four-year programs, PAs often garner more prestige, money, and authority. There have been frequent conflicts when nurses have resented taking orders from PAs. A court suit on that issue was settled in 1980 in the state of Washington. Nurses suffered a serious defeat when the judge made it official that Registered Nurses must take orders from Physicians' Assistants.

In 1988, despite strong objections by the American Nurses' Association, the AMA launched a two-year program for "registered care technologists" to make up for a shortage of nurses. The nurses' ANA indignantly explained to the AMA that more women would choose a nursing career if working conditions and pay scales improved.

Recently, the Graduate Medical Education National Advisory Committee created by the Secretary of Health and Human Services announced an oversupply of physicians by as much as 70,000.[25] This could mean that some of the professional tasks finally given to nurses will be handed back to physicians. Nurse practitioners may find themselves the victims of a concerted effort to drive them out of business. They are already at increased risk of arrest, trial, and imprisonment for "practicing medicine without a license." Some insurance companies have refused to sell them malpractice insurance or have raised premiums so high that they have been forced to close their offices.

Organized opposition has begun to confront the contemporary midwives just as it did their nineteenth-century forerunners. Women who have complications after giving birth have reported that they are sternly lectured about choosing a midwife instead of an obstetrician. Doctors who consent to provide the legally required backup to a midwife have sometimes lost their hospital privileges or find it suddenly difficult to obtain insurance coverage. Although only 6 percent of nurse-midwives have ever been sued, compared with almost 67 percent of obstetricians who have been sued at least once, nurse-midwives find that insurance companies make it difficult and sometimes even impossible to obtain the necessary malpractice coverage. Recently some formed their own mutual insurance company at a cost of about five thousand dollars a year in order to get around this problem.[26]

The rebirth of feminism in the 1970s did not reverse the psychological consequences of hundreds of years of sex role stereotyping. Back in 1876, in an essay competition that concealed the names and sex of contestants from the awards committee, Dr. Mary Putnam Jacobi won Harvard Medical School's esteemed Boylston prize for her paper, "The Question of Rest for Women During Menstruation." Using data based on case studies, she demonstrated that most women performed their normal tasks during their menstrual periods. Almost a century later in 1970, as women took to the streets to demand equality, and as cigarette ads proclaimed, "You've come a long way, Baby!" the same old myth about the physiologic limitations of women persisted in high places. Dr. Edgar Berman, who was Vice-President Hubert Humphrey's physician, stated that "women could not fill leadership roles because of the influences of . . . their menstrual cycles and menopause."[27]

Even when there were more women doctors in clinics and hospitals, the image of doctors as males persisted. Throughout Vanessa Gamble's career, she has all too often heard the comment, "Oh, you're the doctor? I thought you were the nurse."[28]

In a 1974 study of New York City medical and dental clinic patients, 80 percent stated their preference for male physicians, although half of them had never been treated by a woman doctor![29]

Many first-year high school teenage girls who consider a career in medicine are discouraged by the negative attitudes of family members, boyfriends, and guidance counselors. Only 8 percent still have the same ambition by senior year. Perhaps this can be explained by the related findings that indicate even those who graduate with high grades have a lower opinion of their own intelligence than young men with similar honors.

Those who go on to medical school and drop out say that social reasons discouraged them. Women medical students have been shown to have far more anxieties than male students. They worry that they will not be able to handle a family and a medical career. They know full well that most married career women are responsible for the lion's share of household tasks and child care. When men leave medical programs, they usually give academic pressures as their reason for quitting.

Just a few years after they went into effect, affirmative action programs for minorities and women were widely attacked in the press and the courts as being a form of "reverse discrimination." If these programs are abandoned, women will be once again at the mercy of male educators' quotas.

On the other hand, possible "feminization" of medicine could cause more subtle problems. With the supposed excess of physicians, male enrollments in medical schools have recently decreased. As tuition fees skyrocket and opportunities for higher-paying positions become scarcer, men choose more lucrative careers. If the male-female ratio of medical students continues to change, the feminization of medicine is far from impossible. Judging from the European experience, this could lead to a downgrading in the status of doctors and the size of their paychecks.

This is exactly what happened in pharmacy. As more women chose this profession, the owners and managers of the largest employers, the drug chains, realized quickly that they could offer lower salaries to women. Then, of course, as fewer men applied, women pharmacists more and more took on the image of salesclerks, helping customers find their favorite brand of toothpaste or shampoo.

The American Dental Association has stated in their publications that dentistry is ideal for women because of flexible schedules that make it easier to juggle family and professional life. Nevertheless, women are still actively encouraged to enroll in dental auxiliary programs to train as dental assistants and hygienists and not particularly urged to become dentists.

With less encouragement, poorer chances of advancement, and lack of confidence in their own abilities, far fewer women study for advanced degrees in the health professions. Among the so-called new health professionals, the majority of females are employed in the less-skilled, lower-paying jobs.[30]

Professional opportunities for African Americans and other minorities have certainly increased since the civil-rights legislation of the 1960s. It must be remembered, however, that these groups were starting pretty much at ground zero. The growth of the new health professions created some openings for black men who had been trained as medical corpsmen in the armed forces. Black and Hispanic women, however, continue to be most predominant in the lowest-paid service sectors of the health system.

In the professions, the Bureau of the Census categorizes Black Americans, Hispanics, Asians and Pacific Islanders, and a grouping of American Indians, Eskimos and Aleuts as racial/ethnic minorities in the order of their percentage of the population. According to the latest government statistics,[31] all of these minority groups except Asian-Americans are underrepresented in the health professions. In 1990, out of 121,247 women physicians, there were fewer than 6,000 Hispanics, 7,167 African

Americans, 214 Native Americans, Eskimos, and Aleutians, and 18,671 Asians. From 1978–79 until 1984–85, the number of male and female minorities in medicine had grown *less than 1 percent.*[32] Another government document comments:

> *In spite of many efforts to increase the number of minorities in medical schools, the rate of increase in the number of minority entrants, enrollees and graduates has actually declined since the mid-seventies.*[33]

Minority women made greater gains than minority men in their representation in medical schools until 1979, when their comparative rate of enrollment also declined. Black Americans were over 12 percent of the population in 1985, but only 3 percent of them were physicians. Hispanics suffer from a similar disparity. The figures for minority dentists, optometrists, and pharmacists are even lower.

Asians were no longer categorized in 1990 as an underrepresented minority group by the Department of Health and Human Services. Although Asians were only 2.7 percent of the population in 1988, they made up 12.4 percent of first-year medical school classes.

Percentages are not as dramatic as actual numbers. Out of over half a million physicians in the United States, only 15,600 were black and 17,600 were Hispanic. Skyrocketing educational costs and lack of federal aid to education, particularly the cuts of the Reagan administration in government-guaranteed college loans, most severely affected minority groups, whose incomes are well below those of whites. Deterioration of the public school system has been far worse in inner-city ghettos than in predominantly white neighborhoods. Asian immigrants who make the long expensive journey to the United States are often financially better off upon arrival than either black or Hispanic Americans who have been here for generations.

The final report of a forum for college deans in the health professions held in March 1986 stated bluntly that progress in the recruitment of disadvantaged individuals in the health professions "has leveled off and in some cases regressed."[34] Participants from the national Educational Testing Service went further, calling the situation a "crisis in medical education in regard to minority participation." Other deans linked the health problems of black and Hispanic Americans to the shortage of minority physicians.[35]

Apparently, these educators were not exaggerating the extent of the problem. Seven years after their meeting, in 1993, headlines announced a "Big Health Gap, tied to income, is found in U.S." Citing a government report, the article went on to describe a "gap between the mortality rate for blacks and the rate for whites [that] has widened over the last 10 years. . . . Among various income groups, the degree of inequality in mortality rates more than doubled from 1960 to 1986."[36] With the clear and present need for more black and Hispanic doctors apparent, the rate of minority enrollment in medical schools continues to decline.

In the absence of the pressure of organized movements, alarming reports and statistics are quickly filed away. After its early victories, the women's movement, along with the other movements of the 1960s, shrank considerably. Only when the right to a legal abortion was threatened could NOW and other organizations mobilize thousands of women to demonstrate to preserve their hard-won gains.

The women's health movement in the 1980s and 1990s concentrated its energies on what it called "male-oriented" medical research and discrimination against female patients. It criticized the fact that most National Institutes of Health-funded research projects did not include a single woman in the studies.[37] Almost all research on the use of aspirin for the prevention of heart attacks has used male subjects. Physicians have no way of knowing if aspirin therapy would be useful for female heart patients.[38] Even more dangerous, women in need of kidney transplants are far less likely to receive them than men, and older women have half the chance of younger ones of receiving them.[39]

The women health activists scored an important victory when the Women's Health Equity Act became law in 1990. Soon after that, the National Institutes of Health announced a new program called the Women's Health Initiative for research on controversial therapies for women such as Estrogen Replacement Therapy (ERT).[40]

The pre-1980s women's health movement had tried to educate women on the fact that menstruation, pregnancy, and menopause are natural events and should not be treated as diseases. It had resisted the 1960s definition of menopause as a hormone deficiency disease[41], a definition that coincided suspiciously with the time when synthetic hormones like estrogen became widely available. ERT was prescribed for millions of women, with the claim that it would help them to stay "feminine." Despite studies showing a link between ERT and several diseases including endometrial and breast cancer,[42] estrogen remains one of the most widely prescribed drugs for women today.

The medical-care system has been under sharp attack for the poor health status of the American people. Several studies and news reports indicate that women doctors are more nurturing and compassionate than men and therefore are better suited to transform the health-care system.[43]

Dr. Mary Howell, the ex-Harvard Medical School associate dean, disagrees. As she told author Gena Corea, she believes that female doctors have become "honorary white males."

If you're a member of an oppressed group, and you don't see it, you block the ability to see other kinds of oppression too. These women may be even less feeling than men about patients' rights, and the rights of blacks and poor people.[44]

Mary Roth Walsh sounded the alarm fifteen years ago. Referring to the open-door/closed-door phenomenon of the nineteenth century, she called the last chapter of her influential study on women in medicine Will History Repeat Itself?[45] In it she expressed the belief that although the present "small number of women physicians are not going to effect a rapid reform of American medicine . . . it can serve as a base for future improvement." She urged women physicians to "develop attitudes that do not mirror the male-dominated view of medicine" and further encouraged them to "recognize the debt they owe to the feminist movement . . . to remind them of the need for a permanent support group—a politically active women's movement."[46]

Fifteen years after Walsh wrote those words, there was still no mass movement on the scene, yet to many, the need is even greater than it was in 1977. A strong women's-rights movement could play a watchdog role, ready to spring into action long before doors are once again shut and locked tightly. It could encourage all women, including those in medicine, not only to better themselves but also to work to reverse the problems of poverty, racism, environmental destruction, educational decay, homelessness, and so many others that are eroding our world. Men who want a cleaner and healthier world of equality for all people must join in the struggle.

The world of science has been called a "world without women."[47] Most people want a world of men *and* women, joining together to create a better place for people of all races and cultures.

SOURCE NOTES

Chapter One

1. Quoted in David F. Noble, *A World Without Women* (New York: Alfred A. Knopf, Inc., 1992), p. 207.
2. Jeanne Achterberg, *Woman as Healer* (Boston: Shambhala Publications, Inc., 1990), pp. 156–57.
3. For a fuller accounting of this period, *see* Achterberg, pp. 14–58 and Geoffrey Marks and William K. Beatty, *Women in White* (New York: Charles Scribner's Sons, 1972), pp. 41–43.
4. Quoted in Achterberg, p. 16.
5. Quoted in Achterberg, p. 30.
6. Quoted in Achterberg, pp. 39–40.
7. Quoted in Achterberg, p. 50.
8. Noble, pp. 208–9.
9. Quoted in Gena Corea, *The Hidden Malpractice* (New York: Harper and Row Publishers, Inc:, 1977), p. 23.
10. For more details on the Inquisition, *see* Achterberg, pp. 82–98.
11. Quoted in Corea, p. 23.
12. Bobette Perrone, H. Henrietta Stockel, and Victoria Krueger, *Medicine Women, Curanderas, and Woman Doctors* (Norman, Oklahoma: University of Oklahoma Press, 1989), p. 172.
13. Quoted in Achterberg, pp. 87–88.
14. Quoted in Achterberg, pp. 82.
15. Quoted in Achterberg, p. 85.
16. Quoted in Achterberg, p. 86.
17. Corea, p. 22.

Chapter Two

1. Quoted in Howard Zinn, *A People's History of the United States* (New York: HarperCollins Publishers, 1990), p. 103.
2. "Training" usually meant a year or two of attendance at medical schools in Europe, where Galen's primitive theories and therapies such as leeching and purging were taught, or apprenticeship with a physician who had attended such a school.

3. Gena Corea, *The Hidden Malpractice* (New York: Harper and Row Publishers, Inc., 1985), p. 23.
4. Zinn, pp. 107–8.
5. The list includes a "Dr." Millikin of Mount Desert, Maine; Katherine Hebden, the wife of a coffin maker, who recorded that she received a large quantity of tobacco in exchange for her "chirgery [surgery] upon the legg of Dr. John Greenwell . . ."; "Doctress" Joanna Smith, a cousin of the unfortunate Anne Hutchinson; Mrs. Ann Eliot of Roxbury, Massachusetts; and Mrs. Allwyn, who apparently worked as an army surgeon. These names are cited in Helen I. Marieskind, *Women in the Health System* (St. Louis: C. V. Mosby, 1980), p. 121; and Geoffrey Marks and William K. Beatty, *Women in White* (New York: Charles Scribner's Sons, 1972), pp. 76–77.
6. Mary Roth Walsh, *"Doctors Wanted: No Women Need Apply"* (New Haven: Yale University Press, 1977), p. 5.
7. Chadwick Hansen, *Witchcraft at Salem* (New York: George Braziller, 1965), pp. 1–3.
8. For a more detailed description of the Salem events, *see* Larry Gragg, "Under an Evil Hand," in *American History Illustrated* (March/April 1992): pp. 54–59.
9. Quoted in Walsh, p. 7.
10. Zinn, p. 49.
11. The above section on midwives summarizes information contained in Marieskind, pp. 119–21; Jeanne Achterberg, *Woman as Healer* (Boston: Shambhala Publications, Inc., 1990), pp. 126–29; and Walsh, pp. 5–7.
12. Bobette Perrone, et al., *Medicine Women, Curanderas, and Women Doctors* (Norman, Oklahoma: University of Oklahoma Press, 1989), p. 22.
13. *See* Laurel Thatcher Ulrich, *The Life of Martha Ballard, Based on Her Diary, 1785–1812* (New York: Vintage Books, 1991).
14. Ulrich, p. 256.
15. Corea, p. 24.
16. Walsh, p. 5.
17. Quoted in Marks, p. 77.
18. Quoted in Zinn, p. 109.

Chapter Three

1. Quoted in Mary Roth Walsh, *"Doctors Wanted: No Women Need Apply"* (New Haven: Yale University Press, 1977), p. 9.

2. The Cult of Domesticity was also called "The Cult of True Womanhood." For a further description of this period, see Howard Zinn, *A People's History of the United States* (New York: HarperCollins Publishers, 1990), pp. 110–15; Jeanne Achterberg, *Woman as Healer* (Boston: Shambhala Publications, Inc., 1990), pp. 133–36.

3. Barbara Ehrenreich and Deirdre English, *Witches, Midwives, and Nurses–A History of Women Healers* (Old Westbury, New York: The Feminist Press, 1973), pp. 21–22.

4. For more details on the Irregular sects, see Rima D. Apple, ed., *Woman, Health, and Medicine in America* (New York: Garland Publishing, Inc., 1990), pp. 283–88.

5. Zinn, pp. 114–15.

6. Quoted in Zinn, p. 118.

7. For a fuller account, see Zinn, p. 120.

8. Walsh, pp. 19–20.

9. Walsh, p. xii.

10. For a fuller accounting, see Geoffrey Marks and William K. Beatty, *Women in White* (New York: Charles Scribner's Sons, 1972), pp. 73–75; and Carlotta Hacker, *The Indomitable Lady Doctors* (Toronto: Clarke, Irwin & Co., Ltd., 1974), p. 3.

11. Marks and Beatty, pp. 79–81. Lydia Folger Fowler is considered by some to be America's first woman doctor. Because she received her education in an Irregular medical school and Elizabeth Blackwell attended an allopathic school, others give that honor to Blackwell.

12. Quoted in Bobette Perrone, H. Henrietta Stockel, and Victoria Krueger, *Medicine Women, Curanderas, and Women Doctors* (Norman, Oklahoma: University of Oklahoma Press, 1989), p. 128.

13. Quoted in Marks, p. 84.

14. Quoted in Walsh, pp. 31–32.

15. Quoted in Gena Corea, *The Hidden Malpractice* (New York: Harper and Row Publishers, 1985), p. 27.

16. Quoted in Beatrice S. Levin, *Women in Medicine* (Metuchen, New Jersey: The Scarecrow Press, Inc., 1980), p. 73.

17. For more on Zakrzewska, see Levin, pp. 64–66; Walsh, pp. 57–60; and Achterberg, pp. 153–54.

18. For more details on the New England Female Medical College, see Achterberg; p. 131; Marks, p. 77; and Walsh, p. 35.

19. Marks and Beatty, pp. 107–9; Achterberg, p. 148; Levin, p. 96.

20. Quoted in Ruth J. Abrams, ed., *"Send Us a Lady Physician"* (New York: W. W. Norton and Co., Inc., 1985), p. 85.
21. Quoted in Abrams, p. 86.
22. Achterberg, p. 147.
23. For more on Mary Putnam Jacobi, *see* Levin, pp. 96–102.
24. Quoted in Corea, p. 52.
25. Quoted in Corea, p. 51.
26. For more information on Lozier, *see* Corea, pp. 49–52.
27. For fuller details, *see* Corea, p. 26.
28. Quoted in Perrone, p. 127.
29. For more information on Walker, *see* Perrone, pp. 126–28; Levin, pp. 69–71.
30. Women and minorities are often called "separatists" unfairly. Banned from institutions or treated as inferiors inside of them, they frequently want to preserve their own institutions. Most would be more than happy to "integrate" if they believed they would receive equal treatment by the group in power.

Chapter Four

1. Quoted in Geoffrey Marks and William K. Beatty, *Women in White* (New York: Charles Scribner's Sons, 1972), pp. 112–13.
2. Ruth J. Abrams, ed., *"Send Us a Lady Physician": Women Doctors in America, 1835–1920.* (New York: W. W. Norton and Co., Inc., 1985), pp. 157–58.
3. Gloria Moldow, *Women Doctors in Gilded-Age Washington* (Urbana: University of Illinois Press, 1987), p. 8.
4. For a thorough study of this period, *see* Moldow.
5. Quoted in Moldow, p. 61.
6. Quoted in Moldow, p. 60.
7. Jeanne Achterberg, *Woman as Healer* (Boston: Shambhala Publications, Inc., 1990), pp. 155–56.
8. Mary Roth Walsh, *"Doctors Wanted: No Women Need Apply"* (New Haven: Yale University Press, 1977), pp. 199–200.
9. Marks, p. 115.
10. Quoted in Walsh, p. 180.
11. Gena Corea, *The Hidden Malpractice* (New York: Harper & Row Publishers, Inc., 1977), p. 52.
12. Achterberg, p. 156.
13. Quoted in Moldow, p. 33.
14. For more on women doctors abroad, *see* Beatrice S. Levin, *Women and Medicine* (Metuchen, New Jersey: The Scarecrow Press, Inc., 1980), pp. 33–47.

15. Quoted in Rima D. Apple, ed., *Women, Health, and Medicine in America* (New York: Garland Publishing, Inc., 1990), p. 178.

Chapter Five

1. Quoted in Mary Roth Walsh, *"Doctors Wanted: No Women Need Apply"* (New Haven: Yale University Press, 1977), p. 263.
2. For more information on Hispanic midwives and healers, *see* Bobette Perrone et al., *Medicine Women, Curanderas, and Women Doctors* (Norman, Oklahoma: University of Oklahoma Press, 1989), pp. 85–97.
3. For more information on midwifery, *see* Judy Barrett Litoff, "Mid-wives and History," in Rima D. Apple, ed., *Women, Health, and Medicine in America* (New York: Garland Publishing, Inc., 1990), pp. 443–58.
4. Helen I. Marieskind, *Women in the Health System* (St. Louis: C.V. Mosby, 1980), p. 121.
5. *See* table in Walsh, p. 193.
6. Walsh, p. 185.
7. Beatrice S. Levin, *Women in Medicine* (Metuchen, New Jersey: The Scarecrow Press, Inc., 1980), pp. 33–34.
8. For a full presentation of Walsh's arguments, *see* Walsh, pp. 199–202.
9. Quoted in Walsh, pp. 188–89.
10. For further information, *see* Mary V. Dearborn, *Love in the Promised Land* (New York: The Free Press, 1988), pp. 45–47.
11. Quoted in Dearborn, p. 43.
12. Quoted in Walsh, p. 190.
13. Quoted in Jeanne Achterberg, *Woman as Healer* (Boston: Shambhala Publications, Inc., 1990), pp. 156–57.
14. Walsh, p. 201.
15. For more details, *see* Gloria Moldow, *Women Doctors in Gilded-Age Washington* (Urbana: University of Illinois Press, 1987), p. 71.
16. Quoted in Ruth J. Abrams, ed., *"Send Us a Lady Physician"* (New York: W.W. Norton and Co., Inc., 1985), p. 236.
17. For details, *see* Achterberg, pp. 173–75
18. Data is adapted from *Minorities and Women in the Health Fields* (U.S. Department of Health and Human Services, 1990), p. 107.
19. *See* for example, Moldow, pp. 24–25.
20. *See* Moldow, pp. 138–39.
21. Quoted in Walsh, p. 213.
22. For more details about this period, *see* Bettina Aptheker,

Woman's Legacy (Amherst: University of Massachusetts Press, 1982), pp. 64–66.

23. For more details, *see* Walsh, pp. 207–24.
24. Quoted in Walsh, p. 222.
25. Walsh, p. 219.
26. Abrams, ed., p. 227.
27. Walsh, p. 224.
28. For details, *see* Nancy Romer, *The Sex-Role Cycle* (Old Westbury, New York: The Feminist Press, 1981), pp. 12–14.
29. For example, *see* Walsh, p. 250.
30. *See* Walsh, p. 228.
31. Walsh, p. 230.
32. Walsh, p. 234.
33. Walsh, pp. 242–43.
34. Walsh, pp. 245–46.
35. Levin, pp. 51–52.
36. Levin, pp. 55–56.
37. Levin, p. 2.
38. Quoted in Walsh, p. 235.

Chapter Six

1. Quoted in Bettina Aptheker, *Woman's Legacy* (Amherst: University of Massachusetts Press, 1982), p. 110.
2. Other minority women, such as Hispanics, Asians, and Native Americans, also suffered generations of discrimination. However, their stories have scarcely been documented. For example, the Women's Medical College of Philadelphia has only recently launched a research project to reveal the history of Asian women in medicine.
3. Except, where otherwise noted, much of the information in this chapter is based on Herbert M. Morais, *The History of the Negro in Medicine* (New York: Publishers Co., Inc., 1967), pp. 8–28.
4. Aptheker, p. 96.
5. Morais, p. 12.
6. Quoted in Morais, p. 15.
7. Mary Roth Walsh, *"Doctors Wanted: No Women Need Apply"* (New Haven: Yale University Press, 1977), pp. 115–16; Gena Corea, *The Hidden Malpractice* (New York: Harper and Row Publishers, Inc., 1990), p. 85.
8. Quoted in Morais, p. 43.
9. The information on Howard University is described in more detail

in Gloria Moldow, *Women Doctors in Gilded-Age Washington* (Urbana: University of Illinois Press, 1987), pp. 46–47.

10. Quoted in Aptheker, p. 95.
11. Aptheker, p. 99.
12. Stewart M. Brooks, *Our Murdered Presidents* (New York: Frederick Fell, Inc., 1965) pp. 43–45.
13. For more details *see* Jessie Carney Smith, ed. *Notable Black Women* (Detroit: Gale Research, Inc., 1992), pp. 923–24; Aptheker, p. 100; and Ruth J. Abrams, ed., *"Send Us a Lady Physician"* (New York: W.W. Norton and Co., Inc., 1985), p. 107.
14. Aptheker, p. 101; Smith, p. 924.
15. Smith, pp. 290–91.
16. Smith, pp. 261–62.
17. Smith, pp. 923–26.
18. Smith, pp. 401–2.
19. Aptheker, p. 91.
20. Aptheker, p. 99.
21. Smith, p. 924.
22. Smith, pp. 401–2.
23. Brooks, pp. 78–80.
24. Reproduced in full in Morais, pp. 222–23.
25. Quoted in Morais, p. 226.
26. Quoted in Abrams, p. 115.
27. Quoted in Morais, p. 89.
28. Rima D. Apple, ed., *Women, Health, and Medicine in America* (New York: Garland Publishing, Inc., 1990), pp. 491–92.
29. Abrams, p. 107.
30. For further details, *see* Aptheker, pp. 99–103.
31. For details on black women physicians in Washington, D.C., *see* Gloria Moldow, *Women Doctors in Gilded-Age Washington* (Urbana: University of Illinois Press, 1987), pp. 92–93, 111–13, and 130–32.

Chapter Seven

1. Quoted in Barbara Ehrenreich and Deirdre English, *Witches, Midwives, and Nurses* (Old Westbury, New York: The Feminist Press, 1973), p. 36.
2. For more detailed information on the early history of nursing, *see* Geoffrey Marks and William K. Beatty, *Women in White* (New York: Charles Scribner's Sons, 1972), pp. 151–160.
3. Quoted in Marks, pp. 151–52.
4. Quoted in Marks, p. 159.

5. Based on Marks, pp. 151–60.
6. For details on Nightingale's life, *see* Marks, pp. 161–74.
7. Quoted in Marks, p. 168.
8. Quoted in Jeanne Achterberg, *Woman as Healer* (Boston: Shambhala Publications, Inc., 1990), p. 160.
9. Quoted in Gena Corea, *The Hidden Malpractice* (New York: Harper and Row, 1977), p. 58.
10. Quoted in Carlotta Hacker, *The Indomitable Lady Doctors* (Toronto: Clarke, Irwin & Co., Ltd., 1974), p. 10.
11. Rima D. Apple, ed., *Women, Health, and Medicine in America* (New York: Garland Publishing, Inc., 1990), pp. 459–60.
12. Helen I. Marieskind, *Women in the Health System* (St. Louis: C.V. Mosby, 1980), p. 126; and Rosalyn Baxandall, Linda Gordon, and Susan Reverby, eds., *America's Working Women* (New York: Random House, Inc., 1976), pp. 75–77, 346–50.
13. For more details on Dix's life, *see* Marks, pp. 175–87.
14. Quoted in Beatrice S. Levin, *Women and Medicine* (Metuchen, New Jersey: The Scarecrow Press, Inc., 1980), p. 69.
15. Quoted in Apple, p. 461.
16. *See* Apple, pp. 462–63.
17. For more details, *see* Corea, pp. 58–61.
18. Quoted in Mary Roth Walsh, *"Doctors Wanted: No Women Need Apply"* (New Haven: Yale University Press, 1977), p. 142.
19. Quoted in Walsh, p. 143.
20. Corea, p. 59.
21. Achterberg, pp. 175–76.
22. Marieskind, p. 127.
23. For the full story, *see* Corea, pp. 118–26.
24. Herbert K. Morais, *The History of the Negro in Medicine* (New York: Publishers Co., Inc., 1967), p. 250. For a more detailed history of black nurses, *see* Morais, pp. 70–74, 100–2, 139–40.
25. Quoted in Morais, p. 113.
26. Cited in Morais, p. 128.
27. Morais, p. 250.

Chapter Eight

1. In Sheryl Burt Ruzek, *The Women's Health Movement: Feminist Alternatives to Medical Control* (New York: Praeger Publishers, 1985), p. 53.
2. For more details, *see* Jeanne Achterberg, *Woman as Healer* (Boston: Shambhala Publications, Inc., 1990), pp. 178–80.
3. Quoted in Achterberg, p. 179

4. For details, *see* Gena Corea, *The Hidden Malpractice* (New York: Harper and Row Publishers, 1977), pp. 69–72.
5. For the history of pharmacy, *see* Rima D. Apple, ed., *Women, Health and Medicine in America* (New York: Garland Publishing, Inc., 1990), pp. 497–516.
6. Helen I. Marieskind, *Women in the Health System* (St. Louis: C.V. Mosby, 1980), pp. 136–37.
7. Marieskind, p. 136.
8. For more details, *see* Corea, pp. 257–64.
9. Boston Women's Health Book Collective, *Our Bodies, Ourselves* (New York: Simon & Schuster, 1976; reissued as *The New Our Bodies, Ourselves* in 1984).
10. Recounted in Ruzek, pp. 53–58.
11. Quoted in *The Los Angeles Times*, February 5, 1974.

Chapter Nine

1. Quoted in Regina Markell Morantz, Cynthia Stodola Pomerleau, and Carol Hansen Fenichel, *In Her Own Words, Oral Histories of Women Physicians* (Westport, Conn.: Greenwood Press, 1982), pp. 257–58.
2. Author-participant interviews and observations.
3. Jeanne Achterberg, *Woman as Healer* (Boston: Shambhala Publications, Inc., 1990), p. 185.
4. Mary Roth Walsh, *"Doctors Wanted: No Women Need Apply"* (New Haven: Yale University Press), pp. 269–70.
5. *The Americana Annual 1968* (Americana Corp.), p. 432.
6. *See* table in Walsh, p. 269.
7. Quoted in Morantz, pp. 257–58.
8. Achterberg, pp. 185–86.
9. Helen I. Marieskind, *Women in the Health System* (St. Louis: C.V. Mosby, 1980), pp. 136–37.
10. U.S. Department of Health & Human Services, "Minorities and Women in the Health Fields," 1990, p. 144.
11. U.S. Department of Health & Human Services, "Minorities," p. 98.
12. Quoted in Gena Corea, *The Hidden Malpractice* (New York: Harper and Row Publishers, Inc., 1977), p. 63.
13. For more details, *see* Corea, pp. 63–69.
14. Quoted in Achterberg, pp. 176–77.
15. *See* Achterberg, pp. 179–80.
16. Achterberg, pp. 182–84.
17. Marieskind, pp. 143–44.

18. Susan Faludi, *Backlash* (New York: Crown Publishers, Inc., 1991), pp. 363–64.
19. Faludi, pp. 366–67.
20. Achterberg, pp. 185–86.
21. Quoted in Walsh, p. 281.
22. Marieskind, p. 136.
23. U.S. Department of Health & Human Services, "Minorities," p. 117.
24. CBS Evening News, August 11, 1993.
25. Achterberg, p. 177.
26. Achterberg, pp. 184–85.
27. Quoted in Marieskind, p. 130.
28. Quoted in Morantz, p. 258.
29. Marieskind, p. 133.
30. Marieskind, p. 142.
31. Equal Employment Opportunity 1990 computer file, based on Census data.
32. U.S. Department of Health & Human Services, "Minorities," p. 18.
33. Quoted in U.S. Department of Health & Human Services, "Revitalizing Health Professions Education for Minorities and the Disadvantaged," p. 24.
34. U.S. Department of Health & Human Services, "Revitalizing," p. 4.
35. U.S. Department of Health & Human Services, "Revitalizing," p. 1.
36. *New York Times,* July 8, 1993.
37. Rebecca Dresser, "Wanted: Single, White Male for Medical Research." Hastings Center Report, Jan.–Feb. 1992, pp. 24–29.
38. Paul Cotton, "Is There Too Much Extrapolation from Data on Middle-Aged Men?" *Journal of the American Medical Association,* 263, no. 6, 23 Feb. 1990, pp. 1949–2050.
39. Council on Ethical and Judicial Affairs, American Medical Association, "Disparities in Clinical Decision Making," *Journal of the American Medical Association,* 266, 24 July 1991, pp. 559–62.
40. Joseph Palca, "NIH Unveils Plan for Women's Health Project." *Science,* 254, 8 Nov. 1991, p. 792.
41. Corea, p. 237.
42. Corea, p. 237.
43. *See* Bobette Perrone, H. Henrietta Stockel, and Victoria Krueger, *Medicine Women, Curanderas, and Women Doctors* (Norman, Oklahoma: University of Oklahoma Press, 1989), pp. 129–130. A CBS Evening News report on August 11, 1993, announced that the *New England Journal of Medicine* was about to publish an article confirming that women doctors take the complaints of women patients more seriously than male doctors do and send

them more frequently for potentially life-saving mammography and Pap smears.

44. Quoted in Corea, p. 55.
45. Walsh, pp. 268–83.
46. Walsh, p. 283.
47. *See* David Noble, *A World Without Women* (New York: Alfred A. Knopf, 1992).

BIBLIOGRAPHY

BOOKS

*Abrams, Ruth J., ed. *"Send Us a Lady Physician": Women Doctors in America, 1835–1920.* New York: W.W. Norton and Co., Inc., 1985.

Achterberg, Jeanne. *Woman as Healer.* Boston: Shambhala Publications, Inc., 1990.

Apple, Rima D., ed. *Women, Health, and Medicine in America.* New York: Garland Publishing, Inc., 1990.

Aptheker, Bettina. *Woman's Legacy.* Amherst: University of Massachusetts Press, 1982.

*Baker, Rachel. *America's First Trained Nurse.* New York: Julian Messner, Inc., 1959.

*Baker, Rachel. *The First Woman Doctor.* New York: Julian Messner, Inc., 1963.

Baxandall, Rosalyn, Linda Gordon, and Susan Reverby, eds. *America's Working Women.* New York: Random House, Inc., 1976.

Boston Women's Health Collective. *Our Bodies, Ourselves.* New York: Simon & Schuster, Inc., 1976.

Brooks, Stewart M. *Our Murdered Presidents.* New York: Frederick Fell, Inc., 1965.

*Corea, Gena. *The Hidden Malpractice.* New York: Harper and Row Publishers, Inc., 1977, 1985, 1990.

Dearborn, Mary V. *Love in the Promised Land.* New York: The Free Press, 1988.

Dunlop, Richard. *Doctors of the American Frontier.* Garden City, New York: Doubleday and Co., Inc., 1965.

Ehrenreich, Barbara, and Deidre English. *Witches, Midwives, and Nurses: A History of Women Healers.* Old Westbury, New York: The Feminist Press, 1973.

Faludi, Susan. *Backlash.* New York: Crown Publishers, Inc., 1991.

*Hacker, Carlotta, *The Indomitable Lady Doctors.* Toronto: Clarke, Irwin & Co., Ltd, 1974.

Hansen, Chadwick. *Witchcraft at Salem.* New York: George Braziller, 1965.

*Hayden, Robert C. *11 African-American Doctors*. Frederick, Maryland: Twenty-First Century Books, div. of Henry Holt and Co., Inc., 1992.

Levin, Beatrice S. *Women and Medicine*. Metuchen, New Jersey: The Scarecrow Press, Inc., 1980.

Lightfoot, Sara Lawrence. *Balm in Gilead*. Reading, Massachusetts: Addison-Wesley Publishing Co., Inc., 1988.

Marieskind, Helen I. *Women in the Health System*. St. Louis: C.V. Mosby Co., 1980.

*Marks, Geoffrey and William K. Beatty. *Women in White*. New York: Charles Scribner's Sons, 1972.

Moldow, Gloria. *Women Doctors in Gilded-Age Washington*. Urbana: University of Illinois Press, 1987.

*Morais, Herbert M. *The History of the Negro in Medicine*. New York: Publishers Co., Inc., 1967.

*Morantz, Regina Markell, Cynthia Stodola Pomerleau, and Carol Hansen Fenichel. *In Her Own Words, Oral Histories of Women Physicians*. Westport, Connecticut: Greenwood Press, 1982.

Noble, David F. *A World Without Women*. New York: Alfred A. Knopf, Inc., 1992.

*Perrone, Bobette, H. Henrietta Stockel, and Victoria Krueger. *Medicine Women, Curanderas, and Women Doctors*. Norman, Oklahoma: University of Oklahoma Press, 1989.

*Romer, Nancy. *The Sex-Role Cycle*. Old Westbury, New York: The Feminist Press, 1981.

Ruzek, Sheryl Burt. *The Women's Health Movement: Feminist Alternatives to Medical Control*. New York: Praeger Publishers, 1985.

Sexton, Patricia Cayo. *The New Nightingales*. New York: Enquiry Press, 1982.

Smith, Jessie Carnie, ed. *Notable Black Women*. Detroit: Gale Research, Inc., 1992.

Ulrich, Laurel Thatcher. *A Midwife's Tale*. New York: Vintage Books, 1991.

Walsh, Mary Roth. *"Doctors Wanted: No Women Need Apply."* New Haven: Yale University Press, 1977.

*Zinn, Howard. *A People's History of the United States*. New York: HarperCollins Publishers, 1990.

ARTICLES AND DOCUMENTS

Cotton, Paul. "Is There Too Much Extrapolation from Data on Middle-Aged Men?" *Journal of the American Medical Association* 263, no. 6, (23 Feb. 1990).

Council on Ethical and Judicial Affairs, American Medical Association. "Disparities in Clinical Decision Making." *Journal of the American Medical Association* 266 (July 1991).

Dresser, Rebecca. "Wanted: Single, White Male for Medical Research." Hastings Center Report, Jan.-Feb. 1992.

Gragg, Larry. "Under an Evil Hand." *American History Illustrated,* (March/April 1992): 54–59.

Palca, Joseph. "NIH Unveils Plan for Women's Health Project." *Science* 254 (8 Nov. 1991).

U.S. Department of Health & Human Services. "Minorities and Women in the Health Fields," 1990.

U.S. Department of Health & Human Services. "Revitalizing Health Professions Education for Minorities and the Disadvantaged," 1986.

* Books especially recommended for students.

INDEX

Animal Tales

from

MOTHER GOOSE

Compiled by Stephanie Hedlund
Illustrated by Jeremy Tugeau

magic
wagon

visit us at www.abdopublishing.com

Published by Magic Wagon, a division of the ABDO Group, 8000 West 78th Street, Edina, Minnesota 55439. Copyright © 2011 by Abdo Consulting Group, Inc. International copyrights reserved in all countries. All rights reserved. No part of this book may be reproduced in any form without written permission from the publisher.

Looking Glass Library™ is a trademark and logo of Magic Wagon.

Printed in the United States of America, North Mankato, Minnesota.
102010
012011
♻ This book contains at least 10% recycled materials.

Compiled by Stephanie Hedlund
Illustrations by Jeremy Tugeau
Edited by Rochelle Baltzer
Cover and interior layout and design by Abbey Fitzgerald

Library of Congress Cataloging-in-Publication Data

Animal tales from Mother Goose / compiled by Stephanie Hedlund ; illustrated by Jeremy Tugeau.
    v. cm. -- (Mother Goose nursery rhymes)
  Contents: Nursery rhymes about animals -- Baa, baa, black sheep -- Birds of a feather -- Hey diddle, diddle -- Mary had a little lamb -- Gray goose and gander -- Incey wincey spider -- How much wood would a woodchuck chuck? -- Oh where, oh where -- This little pig -- Three blind mice -- To market -- A wise old owl -- Pop goes the weasel.
  ISBN 978-1-61641-142-8
  1. Nursery rhymes. 2. Animals--Juvenile poetry. 3. Children's poetry. [1. Nursery rhymes. 2. Animals--Poetry.] I. Hedlund, Stephanie F., 1977- II. Tugeau, Jeremy, ill. III. Mother Goose.
  PZ8.3.A54929 2011
  398.8--dc22
  [E]   2010024694

Contents

Nursery Rhymes
About Animals

Since early days, people have created rhymes to teach and entertain children. They were often said in a nursery, so they became known as nursery rhymes. In the 1700s, these nursery rhymes were collected and published to share with parents and other adults.

Some of these collections were named after Mother Goose. Mother Goose didn't actually exist, but there are many stories about who she could be. Her rhymes were so popular, people began using *Mother Goose rhymes* to refer to most nursery rhymes.

Since the 1600s, nursery rhymes have come from many sources. The meanings of the rhymes have been lost, but they are an important form of folk language. Nursery rhymes about animals have long been favorites of children.

Baa, Baa, Black Sheep

6

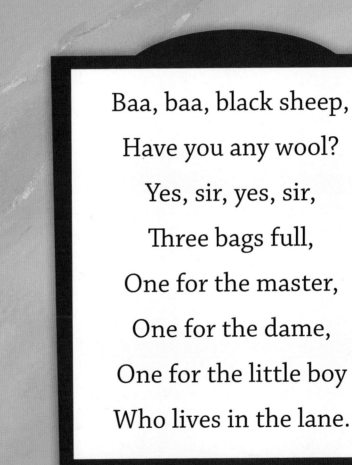

Baa, baa, black sheep,

Have you any wool?

Yes, sir, yes, sir,

Three bags full,

One for the master,

One for the dame,

One for the little boy

Who lives in the lane.

Birds of a Feather

Birds of a feather will flock together,

And so will pigs and swine;

Rats and mice will have their choice,

And so will I have mine.

9

Hey Diddle, Diddle

Hey diddle, diddle,

The cat and the fiddle,

The cow jumped over the moon;

The little dog laughed

To see such sport,

And the dish ran away with the spoon.

Mary Had a Little Lamb

Mary had a little lamb,
Its fleece as white as snow;
And everywhere that Mary went
The lamb was sure to go.

It followed her to school one day,
That was against the rule;
It made the children laugh and play
To see a lamb in school.

And so the teacher turned it out,
But still it lingered near
And waited patiently about
Till Mary did appear.

Why does the lamb love Mary so?
The eager children cry;
Why, Mary loves the lamb, you know,
The teacher did reply.

Gray Goose and Gander

14

Gray goose and gander,

Waft your wings together

And carry

The good king's daughter

Over the one-strand river.

Incey Wincey Spider

Incey wincey spider climbed up the water spout,

Down came the rain and washed poor spider out.

Out came the sun and dried up all the rain;

Incey wincey spider climbed the spout again.

How Much Wood Would a Woodchuck Chuck?

How much wood would a woodchuck chuck

If a woodchuck could chuck wood?

He would chuck as much wood

As a woodchuck could chuck

If a woodchuck could chuck wood.

Oh Where, Oh Where

Oh where, oh where has my little dog gone?

Oh where, oh where can he be?

With his ears cut short and his tail cut long,

Oh where, oh where is he?

This Little Pig

Market →

Wee-
Wee-
Wee!

This little pig went to market,

This little pig stayed home,

This little pig had roast beef,

This little pig had none,

And this little pig cried Wee-wee-wee

All the way home.

Three Blind Mice

Three blind mice, see how they run!

They all ran after the farmer's wife,

Who cut off their tails with a carving knife;

Did you ever see such a sight in your life

As three blind mice?

To Market

To market, to market, to buy a fat pig,

Home again, home again, jiggety-jig;

To market, to market, to buy a fat hog,

Home again, home again, jiggety-jog.

A Wise Old Owl

A wise old owl sat in an oak.

The more he heard, the less he spoke;

The less he spoke, the more he heard.

Why aren't we all like that wise old bird?

Pop Goes the Weasel

All around the cobbler's bench

The monkey chased the weasel;

That's the way the money goes,

Pop goes the weasel!

A penny for a spool of thread,

A penny for a needle;

That's the way the money goes,

Pop goes the weasel!

Glossary

cobbler – a person who fixes shoes.

dame – the woman who is head of a house.

eager – excited or interested.

fleece – the wool coat of an animal, such as a sheep.

gander – an adult male goose.

swine – another name for pig or hog.

waft – to move or go lightly on the air.

Web Sites

To learn more about nursery rhymes, visit ABDO Group online at **www.abdopublishing.com**. Web sites about nursery rhymes are featured on our Book Links page. These links are routinely monitored and updated to provide the most current information available.